Grammar and Punctuation

Grammar 3 Teacher's Guide

Carol Matchett

Schofield&Sims

Free downloads available from the Schofield & Sims website

A selection of free downloads is available from the Schofield & Sims website (www.schofieldandsims.co.uk/free-downloads). These may be used to further enhance the effectiveness of the programme. The downloads add to the range of print materials supplied in the teacher's guides. They include the following items:

- a **Curriculum coverage chart**
- an enlarged **Focus text** for each lesson
- a **Dictation assessment sheet**
- a **Pupil target reminder**
- a **Learning pathways class chart** for each year group
- a **Final test analysis class chart** for each year group.

Published by **Schofield & Sims Ltd**, 7 Mariner Court, Wakefield, West Yorkshire WF4 3FL, UK
Telephone 01484 607080
www.schofieldandsims.co.uk

This edition copyright © Schofield & Sims Ltd, 2017
First published in 2017
Second impression 2019

Author: **Carol Matchett**
Carol Matchett has asserted her moral rights under the Copyright, Designs and Patents Act, 1988, to be identified as the author of this work.

British Library Cataloguing in Publication Data
A catalogue record for this book is available from the British Library.

Design by **Oxford Designers & Illustrators Ltd**

Printed in the UK by **Page Bros (Norwich) Ltd**

ISBN 978 07217 1395 3

Contents

Introduction

Schofield & Sims Grammar and Punctuation is a structured whole-school scheme for teaching grammar and punctuation while also building on vocabulary, reading and writing skills. It can be used alongside the **Schofield & Sims Spelling** series for complete Spelling, Punctuation and Grammar [SPaG] coverage.

Grammar and Punctuation is designed to progressively develop knowledge and understanding of grammatical concepts through six teacher's guides and six pupil books containing a carefully structured sequence of lessons. The teacher's guides provide you, the teacher or adult helper, with notes and activities to support the teaching of these lessons, annotated answers to the pupil book questions, and a variety of assessment resources for tracking progress.

Supporting a mastery approach, the focus of this programme is on rich practice, deep and secure understanding and fluency in application. Pupils not only learn the terminology and correct usage of grammar and punctuation, but they also build up the skills, knowledge and confidence to apply them in their own independent writing. All pupils are encouraged to move at the same pace through the lessons and are given the same opportunity to fully understand the concept being taught. A wealth of practice questions, writing tasks, activity ideas and resources are provided to support the wider application of the grammar and punctuation that has been learnt in each lesson and to help pupils to truly master the art of writing.

The programme is designed primarily for pupils in Years 1 to 6, and the concepts and terminology that are introduced are in line with the National Curriculum for English. However, understanding of grammar and punctuation is cumulative, so grammatical terms and concepts introduced in one book are revisited and developed further in subsequent books to reinforce the pupils' understanding. In particular, concepts and areas of learning introduced towards the end of one book are revisited and embedded in the next book to further ensure consolidation and continuity.

There are 30 corresponding lessons in **Grammar 3** and its related **Teacher's Guide**, ten for each term. These lessons follow the statutory requirements for Year 3 'Vocabulary, grammar and punctuation' in the National Curriculum for English including Appendix 2, while also promoting and supporting other aspects of the English curriculum. A curriculum coverage chart is available to download from the Schofield & Sims website. An extended glossary can also be found at the back of this teacher's guide [pages 91–96], with a full list of all the terminology relevant to the Year 3 curriculum, along with clear explanations, examples and lesson references.

IMPLEMENTING THE TEACHING MODEL

The **Grammar 3 Teacher's Guide** supports explicit teaching of grammar and punctuation within the wider teaching of reading, writing and speaking. It is based on focused teaching sessions, using the following pedagogical model:

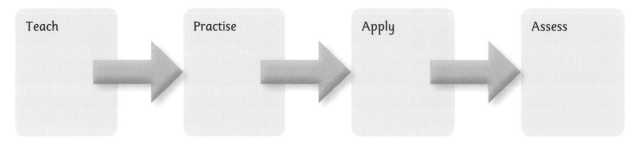

Teach → Practise → Apply → Assess

USING THE TEACHING NOTES

This teacher's guide supports an approach to teaching grammar and punctuation that is systematic, thorough and direct. The teacher's guide provides you with detailed **Teaching notes** for each lesson. A sample page is included below to show the structure of a typical lesson.

Lesson 1 Sentence punctuation

Focus demarcating sentence boundaries with capital letters and full stops; using capital letters for proper nouns

Key terms sentence, capital letter, full stop, proper noun

Focus text Christopher Columbus was an Italian-born explorer who discovered America. In August 1492 he set sail from Spain in his ship the Santa Maria it took a month to cross the Atlantic Ocean there was no sight of land and the crew grew very frightened.

> The learning objective of the lesson.

> Terminology that the pupils will encounter in the lesson.

> A short focus text for use at the start of the lesson.

TEACH

Show the focus text and read it aloud, pausing at the end of sentences – even those not demarcated with full stops [the unmarked sentences end after 'Santa Maria' and 'Atlantic Ocean']. Ask the pupils if the text is punctuated correctly. Do they spot the missing full stops and capital letters? Reread the text, pausing at the end of each sentence to add the capital letters and full stops.

Discuss which other words in the focus text have capital letters. Underline them and ask why they need capital letters [e.g. they are names of people, places, things or months].

Remind the pupils that capital letters and full stops show where sentences start and end. Explain that marking the start and end of sentences is important because it helps to make the meaning of our writing clear. For example, if there were no full stop after the first sentence in the focus text we would not know if Columbus discovered America in August 1492 or set sail from Spain then.

It is important that the pupils are secure in punctuating sentences with capital letters and full stops. If the pupils are still struggling with this, reinforce the process of saying a sentence, writing it with the correct punctuation, then reading and checking the punctuation. Compose another sentence for the focus text to reinforce the process [e.g. They finally sighted land in the West Indies.].

Remind the pupils that capital letters are also used for proper nouns – special names given to specific people, places, things, days of the week and months [e.g. 'ship' is a noun, while 'Santa Maria' is a proper noun – the name of a ship]. Words like 'Italian', which come from a proper noun [Italy], also begin with capital letters.

> Detailed lesson notes offering guidance on how to teach a specific grammatical feature or concept.

EXTEND Discuss other uses of capital letters [e.g. initials; first words in titles].

> Extension of the lesson focus for pupils who want to explore further.

PRACTISE

Pupil book page 4

APPLY

- In all writing across the curriculum, encourage the pupils to orally rehearse a sentence, write it putting in the punctuation and then reread it to check the punctuation.
- Use proofreading partners to make sure that the pupils read aloud their writing, listening for the sentence breaks.
- Ask the pupils to write a given number of sentences on a subject [e.g. three or four sentences under a given sub-heading].
- When writing in other subject areas, focus on capital letters for proper nouns [e.g. in geography – countries, rivers, oceans, cities; in history – people, titles, places, months].

> Reference to the relevant pupil book page, which contains practice activities to develop understanding.

ASSESS

Dictation: Millie went to London on Friday. She saw Buckingham Palace but she did not go inside.
Check: The sentence punctuation is correct and capital letters have been used for proper nouns.

10

> A dictation activity to assess learning.

> Ideas and activities for applying the concept in speech and independent writing.

TEACH

Each lesson begins with an introductory panel featuring the following information:

- **Focus** – The focus of the lesson is clearly stated.
- **Key terms** – The key terminology to be used in the teaching session is listed. Any new terminology that the pupils will come across for the first time in that lesson is highlighted in bold.
- **Focus text** – A short focus text is provided that has been designed for use at the start of the lesson. It is intended that the focus text is written or projected on to a whiteboard to be shared with the pupils. The focus texts cover a range of genres of writing and help to provide a context for the learning that allows the pupils to appreciate the purpose or effect of the target grammar or punctuation feature. All the focus texts are available to download from the Schofield & Sims website.

Clear guidance is given on how to use the **Focus text** at the start of the lesson to 'focus in' on the particular grammar or punctuation feature that you are teaching. The **Teaching notes** suggest possible ways that you can explain, demonstrate and discuss the feature to develop understanding. Sessions often involve some oral composition or shared writing, with the pupils involved in suggesting ideas and correcting mistakes.

The main teaching session covers the objectives that are required for the pupils to work at the expected standard, but there is also a suggestion for how you can **Extend** the focus for pupils who have grasped the main concept and are ready to delve deeper. These suggestions often provide a bridge to later lessons in the programme.

PRACTISE

Following the teaching session, the pupils are ready to practise the grammar or punctuation feature that has been introduced and clear page references are provided for the corresponding lesson in the pupil book. This provides the pupils with rich practice activities to consolidate their learning. The pupils can work individually or in pairs. In paired work, discussion between partners can help to develop understanding, encourage thoughtful answers and promote oral rehearsal.

At the top of each pupil book page a **Remember** panel provides a child-friendly summary of a key learning point from the lesson with examples that refer back to the **Focus text**. This acts as a reminder for the pupil and is also a useful reference for parents if sections of the pupil book are set as homework.

In **Grammar 3**, there are three pupil book activities for each lesson. The first **Try it** activity is designed to check that the pupils understand the key learning point; the second is designed to develop and use this understanding within sentences. You could do some of the activities orally, with the class or in groups, before the pupils write their answers. Each lesson ends with a **Sentence practice** activity where the pupils compose their own sentence or sentences using the concept that has been taught in the lesson. If a pupil requires additional challenge, the **Sentence practice** could be extended by increasing the number of sentences required. A sample page from the pupil book is provided on page 7. It shows the structure of a typical page and some of the main features.

As the pupil book is completed, it will form an ongoing record of the pupil's progress. It will also be a useful reminder for the pupil when writing independently.

Answers to all the pupil book activities are provided in the teacher's guide. Alongside the answers you will also find detailed annotations offering guidance on what to look out for and how to tackle potential problems, as well as suggestions for discussing or comparing the pupils' answers.

There are **Revision** pages at the end of each section of the pupil book. In **Grammar 3**, these pages revise concepts introduced in earlier books as well as material from earlier sections of the current book, making sure that learning is not forgotten. The focus of each revision activity is given on the **Answers** pages in the teacher's guide to help you identify areas where the pupils might need further revision.

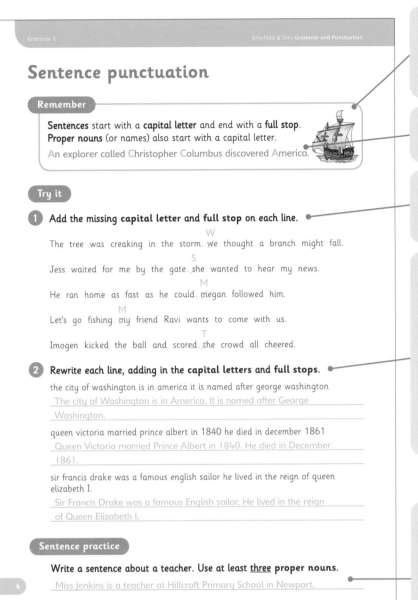

The **Remember** panels provide a child-friendly summary of the key learning point for the page.

Examples are given that refer back to the **Focus text**.

The first **Try it** activity checks for understanding of the key learning point.

The second **Try it** activity develops the pupils' understanding and allows them to practise using the new learning in context. You could do some of these activities orally before the pupils write their own answers [e.g. orally rehearsing sentences or discussing choice of words].

Each lesson ends with **Sentence practice**, where the pupils compose their own sentence or sentences using the key learning point.

APPLY

A challenge when teaching grammar and punctuation is ensuring that pupils transfer learning from grammar lessons into their own writing. This is why the **Teaching notes** always provide a list of suggestions for activities where the pupils might apply their new learning in written, or sometimes oral, composition. These opportunities may be in English lessons or across the curriculum. You can use these suggestions as and when appropriate and you should also look for opportunities to embed learning in the writing activities you already have planned.

It is important to establish the expectation that what has been taught and practised in a grammar and punctuation lesson is applied when writing. This can be helped by setting targets for writing that relate to a specific grammar and punctuation concept that has been taught, and referring to these before, during and after writing, especially in marking and feedback. You will find further support for target-setting on page 9.

At the end of each section of the pupil book there is a short **Writing task**. This again helps to make explicit the link between the grammar and punctuation lessons and the pupils' own writing. The writing task provides an opportunity for the pupils to apply, or 'show off', what they have learnt about grammar and punctuation by using it in written composition. It can be used as a starting point for further creative writing or topic-based activities. There is more information about how to use and assess the **Writing task** on page 8.

ASSESS

Regular assessment is crucial to check understanding, reflect on learning and monitor progress. It is important that teachers know what the pupils have learnt, what they are finding difficult and what they need to know next. This helps inform teaching, planning and target-setting. **Grammar 3** and its related **Teacher's Guide** offer frequent opportunities and a range of resources for in-school assessment, which can be used flexibly in line with your own school's assessment policy.

Ongoing assessment

At the end of each page of the **Teaching notes** you will find a short assessment task based around a dictation exercise. This is designed to be used once the pupils have completed the relevant lesson in the pupil book and begun to apply the new learning in their writing. The pupils are required to write and punctuate a dictated sentence or sentences. They are often then asked to change or annotate the sentences in some way, following verbal prompts. This dictation task is designed to show whether pupils have understood the terminology and the key learning objective of the lesson. Sometimes previous learning is also checked. A **Dictation assessment sheet** is available to download from the Schofield & Sims website.

Periodic assessment

The **Writing task** at the end of each section in the pupil book allows for a more formal assessment of how the pupils are applying their cumulative knowledge of sentence structure, grammar and punctuation in their own writing.

At Key Stage 2, the writing tasks require pupils to write for different purposes and in different forms. You can remind the pupils that you will be looking at their choices of vocabulary, grammar and punctuation but do not give any further help or examples of sentences, words or phrases that might affect the assessment. Allow the pupils a few minutes' planning time to note down their ideas in the space provided before they begin writing.

Included in the teacher's guide is an **Analysis sheet** for each **Writing task** [pages 32, 56 and 80]. This lists relevant criteria relating to punctuation, and to grammar and sentence structure based on what has been taught to date. Look for each criterion in the pupil's completed **Writing task** and record if there is no evidence, some evidence or clear evidence of the use of that feature in the piece of writing. Photocopies of these sheets can also be used to analyse other samples of writing to give a better picture of a pupil's abilities.

Also included is a **Pupil checklist** for each **Writing task** [pages 33, 57 and 81]. This is designed to encourage the pupils' self-assessment and also allows you to give targeted feedback. As the pupils complete the checklist you could ask them to annotate their writing to show where they have successfully used a particular grammar or punctuation feature [e.g. circling the conjunctions they have used].

Whether you choose to use the **Analysis sheet** or the **Pupil checklist**, both include a space for you to record a future target for the pupil. This is an important part of the writing assessments: identifying strengths and weaknesses and informing future teaching. Any problems or misunderstandings that are noted should be addressed and targets updated based on the evidence.

Summative assessment

There is a **Final test** provided as a photocopiable resource on pages 82–85 of this teacher's guide. This is designed to be used as an end-of-year assessment when all or most of the sections of the pupil book are complete. It is similar in style to the short answer test in the end of Key Stage 2 National Tests and it covers all the content introduced in the programme so far. You can use it to help check the pupils' learning and whether their progress is in line with expectations.

A **Mark scheme** for the **Final test** is provided on pages 86–87 and gives the answers and assessment focus of each question. The **Analysis sheet** for the **Final test** allows you to record the marks and will be helpful in identifying individual or class strengths and areas that might need to be revisited. This can be found on page 88 and a whole-class version is available to download from the Schofield & Sims website.

Tracking progress

A number of resources are provided at the back of the teacher's guide and as downloadable resources to further support assessment of learning, tracking progress and record-keeping.

Following a **Writing task**, if a group of pupils require further focused support on a particular writing target, the **Target tracking sheet** on page 89 can be used to note evidence of progress towards that target. You should look for evidence of progress in independent writing in English and in other subjects. Judgements should not be made solely on one piece of writing.

Pupil name	Evidence from independent writing	Progress in independent writing
Sarah Jacobs	Paragraph on 'My family'. Book review of 'The Nightingale'. Science report on 'Habitats'.	① ② ③

The target should be reviewed after a set period of time to see if it has been achieved. A new target might then be set, or further teaching and reinforcement opportunities planned as necessary. A **Pupil target reminder** is available to download from the Schofield & Sims website. This can be placed on a pupil's desk as a prompt to remind them of their current writing target.

The **Learning pathways sheet** on page 90 acts as an at-a-glance overview of where a pupil is in their learning. If completed at regular intervals [e.g. at the end of every term] it allows you to track the progress that has been made and to identify areas where further support might be needed. Alternatively it can be completed just once at the end of the year to act as a useful summative record for the pupil's subsequent teacher. The chart shows criteria in line with the expected standards for Year 3. Circles are ticked to show the depth of a pupil's understanding. These judgements should be made using a variety of evidence, including a number of examples of independent writing. Learning is only definitely embedded when the concept is always or nearly always present based on evidence from a range of writing tasks. A **Learning pathways class chart**, available to download from the Schofield & Sims website, allows you to keep a record of progress for the whole class in one spreadsheet.

The pupils should also be encouraged to reflect on their own learning at regular intervals, saying what they have learnt and how they have used it in their writing. There is a **Progress chart** at the back of the pupil book where the pupils can record their progress through the programme by ticking the circle when they feel they have achieved the content of the statement.

Lesson 1 Sentence punctuation

Focus demarcating sentence boundaries with capital letters and full stops; using capital letters for proper nouns

Key terms sentence, capital letter, full stop, proper noun

Focus text **Christopher Columbus was an Italian-born explorer who discovered America. In August 1492 he set sail from Spain in his ship the Santa Maria it took a month to cross the Atlantic Ocean there was no sight of land and the crew grew very frightened.**

TEACH

Show the focus text and read it aloud, pausing at the end of sentences – even those not demarcated with full stops [the unmarked sentences end after 'Santa Maria' and 'Atlantic Ocean']. Ask the pupils if the text is punctuated correctly. Do they spot the missing full stops and capital letters? Reread the text, pausing at the end of each sentence to add the capital letters and full stops.

Discuss which other words in the focus text have capital letters. Underline them and ask why they need capital letters [e.g. they are names of people, places, things or months].

Remind the pupils that capital letters and full stops show where sentences start and end. Explain that marking the start and end of sentences is important because it helps to make the meaning of our writing clear. For example, if there were no full stop after the first sentence in the focus text we would not know if Columbus discovered America in August 1492 or set sail from Spain then.

It is important that the pupils are secure in punctuating sentences with capital letters and full stops. If the pupils are still struggling with this, reinforce the process of saying a sentence, writing it with the correct punctuation, then reading and checking the punctuation. Compose another sentence for the focus text to reinforce the process [e.g. They finally sighted land in the West Indies.].

Remind the pupils that capital letters are also used for proper nouns – special names given to specific people, places, things, days of the week and months [e.g. 'ship' is a noun, while 'Santa Maria' is a proper noun – the name of a ship]. Words like 'Italian', which come from a proper noun [Italy], also begin with capital letters.

EXTEND Discuss other uses of capital letters [e.g. initials; first words in titles].

PRACTISE

Pupil book page 4

APPLY

- In all writing across the curriculum, encourage the pupils to orally rehearse a sentence, write it putting in the punctuation and then reread it to check the punctuation.
- Use proofreading partners to make sure that the pupils read aloud their writing, listening for the sentence breaks.
- Ask the pupils to write a given number of sentences on a subject [e.g. three or four sentences under a given sub-heading].
- When writing in other subject areas, focus on capital letters for proper nouns [e.g. in geography – countries, rivers, oceans, cities; in history – people, titles, places, months].

ASSESS

Dictation: Millie went to London on Friday. She saw Buckingham Palace but she did not go inside.
Check: The sentence punctuation is correct and capital letters have been used for proper nouns.

Pupil book answers

Sentence punctuation

Remember

Sentences start with a **capital letter** and end with a **full stop**.
Proper nouns (or names) also start with a capital letter.

An explorer called Christopher Columbus discovered America.

Try it

1. Add the missing **capital letter** and **full stop** on each line.

The tree was creaking in the storm. We thought a branch might fall.

Jess waited for me by the gate. She wanted to hear my news.

He ran home as fast as he could. Megan followed him.

Let's go fishing. My friend Ravi wants to come with us.

Imogen kicked the ball and scored. The crowd all cheered.

2. Rewrite each line, adding in the **capital letters** and **full stops**.

the city of washington is in america it is named after george washington

The city of Washington is in America. It is named after George
Washington.

queen victoria married prince albert in 1840 he died in december 1861

Queen Victoria married Prince Albert in 1840. He died in December
1861.

sir francis drake was a famous english sailor he lived in the reign of queen elizabeth I.

Sir Francis Drake was a famous English sailor. He lived in the reign
of Queen Elizabeth I.

Sentence practice

Write a sentence about a teacher. Use at least three **proper nouns**.

Miss Jenkins is a teacher at Hillcroft Primary School in Newport.

4

The pupils will need to recognise that each question contains two sentences. You may wish to point this out to them.

Reading the questions aloud will help the pupils to hear where the first sentence ends and the second one starts.

You could discuss with the pupils why certain words need a capital letter [e.g. name of person, place or month; 'English' because it is from the word 'England'].

This is just an example. The sentence should be correctly punctuated, including capital letters at the start of proper nouns.

In **Grammar 3**, all sentences should be correctly punctuated. Explain this expectation to the pupils.

Lesson 2 Sentence types

Focus revising sentence types and sentence punctuation

Key terms capital letter, full stop, question mark, exclamation mark, punctuation mark, statement, command, question, exclamation

Focus text **Grandpa:**   What a noise! What is it?
Mum: It's Harry. He's learning to play the drums.
Grandma: Please tell him to stop. Take the drumsticks away
from him.

TEACH

Show the focus text. Enjoy reading it aloud with suitable expression, actions and facial expressions.

Ask: How many sentences does each character say? [two] Count the sentences, pointing to the capital letter at the start and the punctuation mark at the end. Ask the pupils to identify the different types of sentence [exclamation, question, two statements, two commands].

Use the focus text to recap the function and patterns of different types of sentence:
* **Statements** tell us something. They usually start with the subject and a verb [e.g. It is ...; He is ...].
* **Questions** ask or request something – they usually need a response. They start with question words [e.g. What is it?] or reordered words [e.g. Is it Harry? Can you tell him to stop?].
* **Exclamations** express emotions and often start with 'What' or 'How' [e.g. What a noise! How awful!].
* **Commands** tell a person to do something. They usually start with the verb and are addressed directly to the person [e.g. Tell him to stop.]. Sometimes they are preceded by words like 'please'.

Remind the pupils that all sentences start with a capital letter and end with a punctuation mark. Questions end with a question mark, exclamations with an exclamation mark, and statements and commands usually with a full stop. Sometimes statements or commands end with an exclamation mark but only to show strong feeling or loudness [e.g. Take the drumsticks away from him!].

Invite the pupils to orally compose and then write another statement, command, question and exclamation for the focus text [e.g. Grandma and Grandpa are here. Stop that now, Harry. Is it always this loud? How awful!].

EXTEND Discuss how to say the same thing using different sentence types [e.g. Stop playing the drums, Harry. Could you stop playing the drums? Or: What a noise! It is very noisy.].

PRACTISE

Pupil book page 5

APPLY

* The pupils write a postcard to a friend, including a question and an exclamation as well as statements.
* The pupils write advertisements using questions, exclamations and commands as well as statements.
* In pairs, the pupils write a script for a lively exchange of dialogue, using different sentence types.
* The pupils write a question or exclamation as the first line of a story to surprise or draw the reader in.
* When revising writing, the pupils check that all sentences end with the correct punctuation mark.

ASSESS

Dictation: <u>Come here</u>. I have a problem. Can you help me? What a good friend you are!
Say: Underline the command.
Check: All sentences are punctuated correctly.

Pupil book answers

Sentence types

Remember

All **sentences** start with a capital letter. **Statements** and **commands** usually end with a full stop, **questions** end with a question mark, and **exclamations** end with an exclamation mark.

What a noise!   Harry is playing the drums.

What is that terrible noise?   Tell him to stop.

Try it

1 Complete each sentence with the correct **punctuation mark**.

Are you coming to see the film _?_ It starts at five o'clock _._

What a great idea _!_ Meet me outside the cinema _._

Did you see the match on Saturday _?_ It was a great game _._

What a result _!_ Do you know who scored the winner _?_

I have fixed the clock _._ What shall I do with it now _?_

How clever of you _!_ Show me how you did it _._

2 Write a **question** or an **exclamation** to follow each sentence. Use the correct punctuation.

Did it rain on your holiday? What _a shame!_

What lovely flowers! What _are they called?_

He gave all his money to charity. How _kind!_

I can't reach the jar on the top shelf. Can _you get it for me?_

I am having an ice cream. Do _you want one?_

Sentence practice

Write <u>three</u> sentences about going camping. Use <u>three</u> different types of sentence.

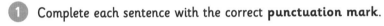

We went camping last week. Have you ever been camping? What an

adventure!

These are just examples of possible questions or exclamations. Apart from in the fourth and fifth sentences, all the answers could be an exclamation or a question. Compare the pupils' answers.

The first word is given to encourage the pupils to form exclamations that start with 'What' or 'How', rather than adding exclamation marks to statements.

The sentences must end with the correct punctuation mark.

5

These are just examples of three possible sentences. The pupils could write a command as one of their sentences [e.g. Come camping with me. Bring a tent.].

The sentences must start with capital letters and end with the correct punctuation mark.

Lesson 3 Noun phrases

Focus expanding noun phrases; using adjectives before and after the noun

Key terms noun, adjective, noun phrase

Focus text A tall, thin man rode into town. He wore a long, shabby coat and a battered hat. At his side he carried a rusty sword with a wooden handle. The man was pale and exhausted.

TEACH

Show the focus text and read it aloud. Discuss the picture created of the stranger. Ask the pupils to identify words and phrases that help create the picture. Underline the noun phrases and adjectives used in the passage [e.g. A tall, thin man; pale, exhausted].

Explain the term 'noun phrase' – a noun [naming word] and the other words that go with that noun, telling us more about it [e.g. 'man' is a noun; 'a tall, thin man' is a noun phrase]. The words 'tall' and 'thin' are adjectives – they tell us more about the noun. More than one adjective is used because each adjective adds something different.

Discuss other noun phrases in the focus text, identifying the nouns and adjectives. Explain that in the description of the sword, there is an adjective before the noun [rusty] and an extra detail after the noun [with a wooden handle]. Details like this are sometimes added to make a longer noun phrase.

Discuss the last sentence. Here the adjectives come *after* the noun [the man was pale]. We know 'pale' is an adjective because it tells us more about the noun [the man]. Explain that when adjectives are added after the noun, a verb is used [e.g. 'was' – it could also be 'seemed' or 'looked'].

Invite the pupils to orally compose other noun phrases about the stranger, using adjectives before and after the noun, and other descriptive phrases [e.g. the man was weak; a tall, thin man with a limp].

EXTEND   Use other words than 'with' to add details after a noun [e.g. on; in; by].

PRACTISE

Pupil book page 6

APPLY

- The pupils write descriptions of another mysterious stranger. Use oral rehearsal to encourage careful choice of nouns and adjectives. Discuss the effect of different words on the meaning.
- When the pupils are writing stories, encourage them to expand noun phrases in different ways to add detail to descriptions of characters, settings, objects or imaginary creatures [e.g. in traditional tales].
- When the pupils are writing instructions, adverts or other non-fiction texts, discuss how adjectives and expanded noun phrases might be used [e.g. to add precision; to specify; to sound persuasive].
- Set a 'two adjectives per noun' rule to discourage overuse of adjectives.
- The pupils write poems using interesting adjectives and expanded noun phrases [e.g. describing the four seasons].

ASSESS

Dictation: The poor farmer lived in a small cottage in the wood.
Say: Underline the two adjectives, and circle the nouns they describe. Rewrite the sentence with two more adjectives.
Answer: e.g. The poor farmer lived in a small pokey cottage in the dark wood.
Check: Look for good choice of adjectives added to any of the nouns.

Pupil book answers

Noun phrases

Remember

You can add **adjectives** to a **noun** to say more about it. This makes a longer **noun phrase**. You can also make a longer noun phrase by adding some detail after the noun.

man (noun)   a tall, thin man (noun phrase)

sword (noun)   a sword with a wooden handle (noun phrase)

These are just examples of how the noun phrases might be completed. Look for choice of appropriate adjectives and descriptive details. Compare the pupils' answers and the different images created.

Sometimes commas are needed to separate two adjectives before a noun. However, this is not a requirement for the pupils at this stage.

Try it

1 Complete each noun phrase using **adjectives** and descriptive details.

the clown's ___funny___ ___long___ shoes

Grandad's ___smart___ ___red___ tie

the ___excited___ ___little___ girl in ___the stripey blue top___

my ___comfortable___ slippers with ___furry insides___

the queen's ___bright___ ___colourful___ dress with ___lacy sleeves___

the ___cute___ ___black___ puppy with the ___big brown___ eyes

2 Use **adjectives** to complete these sentences.

The wood was ___dark___ and ___scary___.

The car looked ___new___ and ___expensive___.

The clouds were ___grey___ and ___stormy___.

The woman was ___old___ and ___wrinkled___.

The prince was ___handsome___ but ___foolish___.

The dragon was ___huge___ but ___friendly___.

Look for two appropriate adjectives. In the first four sentences the two adjectives are joined by 'and', so they should go together. In the last two sentences the two adjectives are joined by 'but', so they should create a contrast. Compare the pupils' choices and the different images created.

Sentence practice

Write a sentence using a longer **noun phrase** to describe a cat.

___A sleek black cat with green eyes prowled the dark street.___

This is just an example. Look for a sentence with one or two adjectives before the noun or an added detail after the noun. The pupils may choose to add adjectives after the noun [e.g. The cat in the street was sleek and black.].

6

Lesson 4 Using 'a' or 'an'

> Focus using 'a' or 'an' in noun phrases
>
> Key terms noun, adjective, noun phrase, **article**, **consonant**, **vowel**
>
> Focus text In the box, I found a diary, an envelope, a train ticket, an old watch and the map I was looking for.

TEACH

Show the focus text and read it aloud. Discuss what items are found in the box, underlining each noun phrase in a different colour [e.g. a diary; an envelope]. Explain that adding the word 'a'/'an' or 'the' before a noun makes it a noun phrase.

Circle the words 'the', 'a' and 'an'. Explain that these familiar little words are called articles. They come before nouns and at the start of noun phrases – *before* any adjectives added to the noun. Tell the pupils that one way of checking if a word is a noun is to put 'the' or 'a'/'an' before the word and see if it sounds right. [Note: Articles are a type of determiner. Determiners will be covered in **Grammar 4**.]

Use the focus text to discuss the difference between 'the' and 'a'/'an' [e.g. 'the box' suggests that it is a particular box, while 'a diary' suggests that it is an unknown diary, or just any diary]. [Note: 'The' is called the definite article because it refers to a definite item, while 'a'/'an' is the indefinite article. However, the pupils do not need to know these terms.]

Look at the circled words. Point out that sometimes 'an' is used instead of 'a'. Ask the pupils if they can work out why. If not, explain that we use 'a' before words beginning with a consonant sound, and 'an' before words beginning with a vowel sound, to make them easier to say [e.g. a envelope/an envelope].

Check that the pupils know the vowel letters [a e i o u] and can recognise long and short vowel sounds. It is vowel *sounds* that determine the use of 'an' rather than 'a'.

Invite the pupils to create a new selection of nouns to put in the box, using 'a' or 'an' appropriately [e.g. Put some fruit in the box: a peach; a banana; an orange; an apple.].

EXTEND Discuss examples such as 'an hour' [it starts with a consonant *letter* but a vowel *sound*, so we use 'an'] or 'a uniform' [it starts with a vowel *letter* but a consonant *sound*, so we use 'a'].

PRACTISE

Pupil book page 7

APPLY

- The pupils write a list of items found in a special 'magical' box or a box belonging to a particular person. Challenge them to use 'an' at least once in their list.
- In other subject areas, ensure the correct use of 'a'/'an' with subject-specific terms [e.g. in maths – an eighth, an octagon; in geography – an ocean, an office block].
- When writing descriptive noun phrases, check that the use of 'a'/'an' is correct [e.g. an old red sock; an odd little man].
- The pupils write lists of items seen or labels for items collected [e.g. an acorn from an oak tree].

ASSESS

Dictation: We need an onion, a carrot and a pumpkin. Do we need an apple or a plum?
Say: Underline all the articles in these sentences.
Check: The sentences are correctly punctuated, including the comma in the first sentence. [Note: Using commas between items in a list is revised in the next lesson, Lesson 5.]

Pupil book answers

Using 'a' or 'an'

> **Remember**
>
> You can use the words 'a' and 'an' before nouns and noun phrases. You use **'a'** before words beginning with a **consonant** sound and 'an' before words beginning with a **vowel** sound.
>
> a <u>d</u>iary   a <u>t</u>rain ticket   an <u>e</u>nvelope   an <u>o</u>ld watch

Try it

1 Write **'a'** or **'an'** before each noun.

_a_ duck	_an_ owl	_an_ eagle	_a_ swan
_an_ inkpot	_a_ stamp	_an_ address	_a_ postcard
_a_ scarf	_an_ umbrella	_a_ jacket	_a_ hood
_a_ toaster	_an_ iron	_an_ apron	_a_ kettle
_an_ arm	_an_ elbow	_a_ hand	_a_ thumb
_a_ nose	_an_ ear	_an_ eye	_a_ mouth

2 Complete the sentences by adding **'a'** or **'an'** before each noun.

Do you want _a_ cake, _an_ ice cream, _an_ orange or _an_ apple?

I need _an_ egg, _a_ tomato, _an_ onion and _a_ red pepper.

I saw _an_ oak tree, _a_ birch, _an_ elm and _a_ willow.

Is _an_ ant _an_ insect or _a_ reptile?

_A_ minute is shorter than _an_ hour but longer than _a_ second.

The circus had _a_ juggler, _an_ acrobat, _a_ clown and _an_ amazing tightrope walker.

There was once _a_ beautiful princess, _an_ ugly prince, _an_ evil monster and _a_ clever witch.

In the fifth sentence, 'hour' is preceded by 'an' because it begins with a vowel *sound* even though 'h' is a consonant letter. Reading the sentence aloud will show this.

Check also that the first 'a' in this sentence is a capital letter.

Sentence practice

Complete this sentence by adding a list of <u>four</u> animals. Use the word 'an' <u>two</u> times.

At the zoo I saw _an elephant, an ostrich, a lion and a tiger._

7

This is an example of a suitable sentence. The pupils could add other animals. The sentence must be correctly punctuated, including the use of commas to separate the animals in a list. There must be no comma before 'and'. [Note: Using commas in lists of noun phrases is revised in the next lesson, Lesson 5.]

Lesson 5 Commas in lists

Focus using commas to separate items in a list of noun phrases and verb phrases

Key terms comma, noun phrase, noun, adjective, verb

Focus text **It was a beautiful garden with tall blossom trees, neat hedges, glittering fountains, brightly coloured flowers and soft green grass. People were sweeping paths, mowing lawns, weeding borders, cutting hedges or planting flowers.**

TEACH

Show the focus text. Read aloud the first sentence. Discuss the items seen in the beautiful garden. Underline each item in a colour [e.g. tall blossom trees; glittering fountains]. Point out that each item is a noun phrase, with nouns and adjectives. Discuss why commas are needed in the sentence [there is a list of items; the commas separate the items in the list].

Read aloud the second sentence. Discuss the actions of the people. Underline each action in a different colour [e.g. sweeping paths; weeding borders]. Discuss why commas are needed in this sentence [because there is a list of actions; the commas separate the actions in the list].

Remind the pupils that commas are used to separate items in a list when there are three or more nouns or noun phrases. A comma is added after each noun or noun phrase except the one before the last item in the list, when the word 'and' is used instead, so usually no comma is needed.

Explain that commas are also used when there is a list of actions, as shown in the second sentence of the focus text. The commas separate the different actions. This sentence also shows that sometimes 'or' is used rather than 'and' [e.g. if it is a list of alternatives].

Invite the pupils to construct another sentence using a list of noun phrases, such as things *not* seen in the garden [e.g. There were no chipped flowerpots, untidy borders, overgrown paths …]. Write the sentence using commas.

EXTEND Construct another sentence with a list of actions, perhaps using a different setting.

PRACTISE

Pupil book page 8

APPLY

- The pupils write a sentence with a list of noun phrases to describe a place or setting in a story [e.g. In the room there were …]. They then write a sentence with a list of actions, for example to describe a busy place such as a city street, a market or a football ground [e.g. People were …].
- In traditional stories, look for sentences listing three noun phrases or three actions [e.g. … a big bear, a grizzly bear, a hungry bear …]. Let the pupils write their own sentences based on these examples.
- The pupils write a sentence describing the ingredients needed for a recipe [e.g. You will need a big mixing bowl, two eggs, …].
- The pupils write list sentences in other curriculum areas [e.g. in science – the diet of animals, descriptions of plants; in design and technology – items required to make something].

ASSESS

Dictation: The fisherman caught a tin can, an old boot, a frog, an eel and an enormous fish.
Check: Commas are correctly placed and 'a' and 'an' are used correctly.

Pupil book answers

Commas in lists

Remember

Commas are used to separate items in a list of words or noun phrases. There is no comma before the last item. You use the word '**and**' (or the word '**or**') instead.

It was a beautiful garden with tall blossom trees, neat hedges, glittering fountains, brightly coloured flowers and soft green grass.

Try it

1 Add the missing **comma** or commas to each sentence.

She felt in her coat pocket and found a green hair ribbon, two squares of chocolate, a clean tissue and her lost glove.

People were chatting, buying popcorn and finding their seats.

The servants cleaned the windows, polished the silver, swept the floors and dusted the furniture.

Squirrels have grey fur, bushy tails, pointed ears and sharp claws.

Do you want a fried egg, a slice of toast, a banana or a bowl of porridge?

> Check that there is no comma before 'and' or 'or'.

2 Complete each sentence by adding <u>three</u> more **noun phrases**. Use the correct **punctuation**.

Inside the room was a comfy chair , a small table, a cosy fireplace and an old grandfather clock.

He decorated the cake with two colours of icing , sugar stars, chocolate sprinkles, candles and a bright red ribbon.

The monster ate six red buses , a black taxi, some old rusty pipes and a set of traffic lights.

> These are just examples of noun phrases that could be added.
>
> Check that commas are used between the noun phrases, except for before 'and'.

Sentence practice

Write a sentence to say what someone in a story was wearing. Include a list of <u>four</u> **noun phrases**.

The wizard wore purple gloves, a pointy hat, shiny boots and a long cloak.

This is just an example of the sort of sentence the pupils might write. It could be about any character in a story. Compare different sentences. Check that commas are used between the noun phrases, except for before 'and'.

Lesson 6   Apostrophes for possession

> Focus   apostrophe for singular possession; distinguishing apostrophes for possession and omission
>
> Key terms   apostrophe, punctuation mark, **contraction**
>
> Focus text   Here's Dad's toolbox. There's Joe's old bike.
> There's the dog's kennel. That's the hamster's cage.
> Where's grandad's walking stick? It's behind Emma's tricycle.

TEACH

Show the focus text and read it aloud. Discuss the items found in the shed, and who or what they belong to. Underline the phrases that tell us this information [e.g. Dad's toolbox; the dog's kennel].

Look at these phrases. Ask the pupils to name the punctuation mark used in each phrase [an apostrophe]. Discuss why it is needed [it shows that something belongs to someone or something].

Discuss the other apostrophes in the focus text [here's, there's, that's]. Why are they used? [to show there is a missing letter in a shortened form] Say each sentence with the full version of the contracted forms [e.g. Here is Dad's toolbox.].

Remind the pupils that there are two different uses of the apostrophe:
* in place of missing letters in shortened forms of words, called contractions. This is where two words are contracted into one [e.g. there is/there's].
* with the letter 's' to show possession – something belongs to someone or something [e.g. Joe's old bike; the hamster's cage]. This is used because it is quicker and neater than saying 'the old bike belonging to Joe' or 'the cage belonging to the hamster'.

Identify examples of each use of the apostrophe in the focus text. For both uses, the words end in the same way, with 'apostrophe s'. Ask the pupils to say whether each one is a contraction of the verb 'is' or if it shows possession.

Invite the pupils to compose more sentences about other items that might be found in the shed [e.g. Here's Katie's old pram.].

EXTEND   Discuss possessive apostrophes with plural nouns [e.g. if there were two hamsters it would be 'the hamsters' cage']. [Note: This is covered in **Grammar 4**.]

PRACTISE

Pupil book page 9

APPLY

* The pupils write lists of lost or found items [e.g. items lost on a school trip; items found in a cupboard].
* The pupils write spells using ingredients with apostrophes [e.g. a bee's sting; an owl's feather].
* Encourage the use of possessive apostrophes when writing about the function of parts of plants or animals [e.g. an elephant's trunk is very useful; a plant's roots …].
* The pupils write descriptions of real or imaginary animals [e.g. an elephant's trunk is like a hose pipe].

ASSESS

Dictation: Anna's going to wash Mum's car. She's going to polish the car's wheels and clean the headlights.
Say: Underline the two words that use an apostrophe to show possession.
Check: All four apostrophes are correctly placed. There should be no apostrophe in 'wheels' or 'headlights'.

Pupil book answers

Apostrophes for possession

Remember

Apostrophes are used in **contractions** or shortened forms of words. **Apostrophes** are also used with the letter 's' to show that something belongs to someone or something. The apostrophe shows possession.

Dad's toolbox   the dog's kennel

Try it

1 Underline the word that has an **apostrophe** to show that something belongs to someone.

I'll put the folders on the <u>teacher's</u> desk.

That's the <u>fisherman's</u> boat over there.

There's a pigeon sitting on the <u>scarecrow's</u> hat.

I can't find the <u>dog's</u> lead anywhere.

Mum's taken <u>Dad's</u> car to the garage.

The <u>boy's</u> arm is in a sling because he's broken it.

2 Rewrite each phrase using an **apostrophe** to show possession.

the easel belonging to the artist   the artist's easel

the nest belonging to the bird   the bird's nest

the burrow belonging to the rabbit   the rabbit's burrow

the stripes of a tiger   a tiger's stripes

the wings of an owl   an owl's wings

the surface of the Earth   the Earth's surface

Sentence practice

Write a sentence about something that belongs to a pirate. Use an **apostrophe**.

The pirate's parrot sat on his shoulder and squawked.

If the pupils have difficulty with this activity, remind them to ask: Is it a contraction of two words? Or does it show a possession – something belonging to someone or something?

You could discuss which two words are contracted [e.g. I will/I'll; that is/that's; there is/there's; Mum has/Mum's].

This is just an example of a sentence showing the use of a possessive apostrophe.

9

21

Lesson 7 Using adjectives to compare

Focus using the suffixes –er and –est or the words 'more' and 'most' with adjectives

Key terms suffix, adjective

Focus text This car is fast but that car is faster.
This car is smooth but that one is smoother.
This car is comfortable but that one is more comfortable.
This car is good but that one is better.

TEACH

Show the first two sentences of the focus text and read them aloud. Discuss the purpose of the sentences [e.g. they are comparing two cars]. Discuss what type of word is highlighted [adjectives – they tell us more about the two cars and how they compare].

Reveal the next two sentences and read them aloud. Discuss the highlighted adjectives Ask: Why don't we say 'comfortabler' or 'gooder' instead? [e.g. these are more difficult to say]

Explain that we use comparative adjectives like these to compare two things. With a short adjective, the suffix –er is usually added [e.g. faster; smoother] but with longer words the word 'more' is used instead [e.g. more comfortable]. This makes it easier to say [e.g. comfortabler/more comfortable]. Discuss other comparative adjectives that use 'more' [e.g. more beautiful; more modern].

Explain that a few adjectives change completely when they are used to compare things [e.g. good/better]. Give another example [e.g. bad/worse – 'This car is bad but that one is worse.', not 'badder'].

Discuss what would happen if there was a third car. Explain that we would use the –est suffix with a short word [e.g. This car is the fastest car of all.], but we would use the word 'most' with a longer word [e.g. the most comfortable car of all]. Ask: What about 'good'? [This car is the best car of all.]

EXTEND Introduce the idea of comparative adverbs [e.g. This car went *fast*. That one went *faster*.].

PRACTISE

Pupil book page 10

APPLY

- The pupils write sentences comparing the best or worst of something, using suitable adjectives [e.g. the best and worst cars, houses, bikes].
- The pupils write fables with contrasting characters, using adjectives to compare them [e.g. finer feathers; a sweeter voice; a more beautiful beak].
- Encourage the use of adjectives when making comparisons in other subjects [e.g. in geography – warmer, cooler, more tropical].
- The pupils use adjectives with –est and 'most' to write about 'the most interesting person I know' or 'the most beautiful place to visit'.

ASSESS

Dictation: I think you will like this book. It is <u>more interesting</u> than that one. It is <u>funnier</u> and has a <u>better</u> ending.
Say: Underline the adjectives that compare the books.
Check: The sentence punctuation is correct.

Pupil book answers

Using adjectives to compare

> **Remember**
>
> You can use **adjectives** to compare things. With short adjectives, add the **suffixes –er** and **–est**.
>
> fast   faster   fastest
>
> With longer adjectives, use the words '**more**' and '**most**'.
>
> comfortable   more comfortable   most comfortable

Try it

1 Complete the table of **adjectives**. Some have been done for you.

Adjective	–er or 'more'	–est or 'most'
smooth	smoother	smoothest
fierce	fiercer	fiercest
hungry	hungrier	hungriest
important	more important	most important
famous	more famous	most famous
surprising	more surprising	most surprising

The adjectives should be spelt correctly, including those that require a change in spelling [e.g. hungrier].

2 Complete each sentence with the correct form of the **adjective**.

This snake is _____ more dangerous _____ than that one.   (dangerous)

Is this the _____ brightest _____ star in the sky?   (bright)

Simon is the _____ happiest _____ boy I know.   (happy)

It was the _____ most beautiful _____ sunset.   (beautiful)

This story is _____ better _____ than your last one.   (good)

Sentence practice

Write a sentence using **adjectives** to compare two fairground rides.

This ride is bigger and more exciting than that one.

Again, check that the adjectives are spelt correctly, including those requiring a change in spelling [e.g. happiest].

If necessary, remind the pupils that 'the' comes before the –est form of the word.

Lesson 8　Conjunctions

Focus　introducing the term 'conjunction' and revising its function

Key terms　**conjunction** [previously 'joining word'], sentence

Focus text　The little girl was worried because she found the cottage door open. She knocked on the door but no-one answered. No-one answered when she knocked a second time. She knocked a third time and this time she heard a gruff voice.

TEACH

Show the focus text and read it aloud. Discuss what story it might be taken from [Little Red Riding Hood]. Discuss what has happened before this moment in the story and what happens next.

Read each sentence, discussing the purpose of the highlighted words [e.g. they are 'joining words'; they join together two separate ideas or sentences to make a longer sentence]. Read the text without the joining words and discuss why it is not as effective [e.g. it sounds disjointed; the ideas do not link together].

Explain that the correct term for a joining word is 'conjunction'. Point out the connection between this word and a road junction, which joins two roads; in grammar, a conjunction joins two parts of a sentence. Conjunctions are used to join two ideas or sentences together to make one longer sentence [e.g. 'The little girl was worried because she found the cottage door open.' = two ideas in one sentence].

Use the sentences in the focus text to discuss how the different conjunctions link ideas [e.g. 'because' adds a reason; 'but' introduces a contrasting or unexpected idea].

Ask the pupils what other conjunctions they know [e.g. or; if; that]. Invite them to orally construct more sentences for the focus text using these conjunctions [e.g. The little girl was surprised because ...; She thought that ...; She could go inside or ...].

EXTEND　You could discuss the difference between co-ordinating conjunctions [and, but, or] and subordinating conjunctions [e.g. when; if; because]. [Note: The terms 'subordinate clause' and 'subordinating conjunction' are introduced in Lesson 22. Co-ordinating conjunctions are introduced in **Grammar 4**.]

PRACTISE

Pupil book page 11

APPLY

- Set the pupils the target of using a wide range of conjunctions in their writing, rather than just 'and' or 'but' [e.g. when; if; because].
- Challenge the pupils to write a story using four different conjunctions and then highlight these to show when and how they have been used.
- When writing in other curriculum areas, encourage the use of conjunctions to clarify the relationship between ideas [e.g. to explain – 'when', 'because', 'if'; to compare and contrast – 'and', 'but'].
- The pupils write list poems or descriptive sentences using sentence stems ending with different conjunctions [e.g. It was so cold that ...; I wonder if ...; I feel sad when ...].

ASSESS

Dictation: Someone was in Grandma's bed <u>but</u> it wasn't Grandma. The little girl thought <u>that</u> it might be a wolf.

Say: Underline the conjunction in each sentence.

Check: All punctuation is correct, including the apostrophes.

Pupil book answers

Conjunctions

Remember

A **conjunction** is a joining word. Conjunctions are used to join together two ideas or two sentences to make one longer sentence.

The little girl was worried because the cottage door was open.

Try it

1 Choose the best **conjunction** from the box to complete each sentence. Use each conjunction only <u>once</u>.

> and   that   but   when   if   or

I went swimming for the first time ____when____ I was four years old.

They tried to go on ____but____ the bad weather forced them back.

She opened the cupboard ____and____ found the cooking pot.

I might go fishing ____or____ I might swim in the sea.

You can come on the trip ____if____ you get here on time.

The doctor told him ____that____ his wrist was broken.

2 Complete each sentence using the **conjunction** in **bold**.

The snowman melted **when** it got too warm.

The day was almost over **but** we did not want to go to bed.

I was hurrying to catch the bus **when** I fell over.

The sheep will escape **if** you leave the gate open.

I'm glad **that** you like the present.

Rachel won the prize **because** her picture was the best.

Sentence practice

Write <u>two</u> sentences about the weather today. Use <u>two</u> different **conjunctions**.

It was raining when I woke up. It is still cloudy now but it is getting a bit brighter.

11

Different conjunctions could be used in some sentences. However, the pupils are asked to use each conjunction only once. You may need to encourage them to choose an alternative conjunction from the box for some sentences.

You could discuss with the pupils which conjunction is the 'best' choice for each sentence.

These are just examples of how sentences might be completed. You could compare the pupils' choices.

The sentences should make sense and be grammatically correct. Look for any inconsistency in use of tense and discuss this with the pupils [e.g. The snowman melted when it gets too warm.].

There should be no capital letter after the conjunction.

This is an example of two sentences using the conjunctions 'when' and 'but'. The pupils could use other conjunctions in their sentences.

Lesson 9 Conjunctions to show time

Focus using conjunctions to express time [e.g. when, before, after, while]

Key terms conjunction

Focus text **Queen Isabella ate a slice of cake** when **she returned to the palace.**

TEACH

Show the focus text. Read the sentence aloud. Discuss what the queen did and when she did it.

Discuss the highlighted word. Decide what type of word it is [conjunction – it joins the two pieces of information given in the sentence]. Replace 'when' with the word 'before'. Read the sentence again. Discuss how this changes the meaning of the sentence [Queen Isabella ate the cake earlier, *before* she returned]. Do the same with the word 'after', discussing how it changes the meaning.

Explain that 'when', 'before' and 'after' are conjunctions that help show *when* an event happened – for example, in relation to another event. They are sometimes called time conjunctions.

Invite the pupils to orally construct their own sentences about when Queen Isabella ate cake, using the conjunctions 'when', 'before' and 'after' [e.g. Queen Isabella ate a slice of cake before she inspected the troops.]. If the pupils suggest sentences with just a word or phrase following the word 'before' or 'after' [e.g. before tea; after supper], point out that sentences like these do not use the words 'before' and 'after' as conjunctions, because a conjunction must be followed by a *clause* with a verb. The pupils will learn more about this in Lesson 21 but, for the moment, help to rephrase such sentences so there is a complete clause after the conjunction [e.g. before she <u>had</u> tea; after she <u>had</u> supper].

Write some more time conjunctions on the board [e.g. while; as; until]. Invite the pupils to orally construct a new set of sentences using these conjunctions [e.g. Queen Isabella was eating a slice of cake while she waited for the king to arrive home.].

EXTEND Introduce other conjunctions that can be used to express time [e.g. once; since].

PRACTISE

Pupil book page 12

APPLY

- When the pupils are writing stories, personal accounts and accounts of events in history, encourage the use of time conjunctions to show when events happened in relation to each other.
- Ask the pupils to highlight the time conjunctions they have used in a story or account.
- Encourage the use of conjunctions when the pupils are writing instructions or advice [e.g. about crossing the road – 'Look both ways before you cross the road. Keep looking as you cross the road.'].
- The pupils write an opening sentence for a story, including a time conjunction [e.g. It all began when ...; I had never been in trouble before ...; I never believed in magic until ...].

ASSESS

Dictation: I was eating my breakfast <u>while</u> Dad was in the shower. The post arrived <u>as</u> I was finishing the last mouthful.
Say: Underline the time conjunction in each sentence.
Check: The sentence punctuation is correct.

Pupil book answers

Conjunctions to show time

Remember

Conjunctions such as '**when**', '**before**', '**after**' and '**while**' help to show <u>when</u> events happen.

Queen Isabella ate a slice of cake before she returned to the palace.

Try it

1 Choose the best **conjunction** to complete each sentence.

I finished my book ____before____ I went to sleep.   (before after while)

Switch off the computer ____when____ you have finished.   (while before when)

I packed my bag ____while____ Mum was waiting.   (after while until)

Wash your hands ____after____ you clean the hamster cage.   (until as after)

They searched the wood ____until____ it was dark.   (as until while)

There was not a sound ____as____ we crept up the path.   (after as before)

These are just examples of how the sentences might be completed. You could compare the different endings added by the pupils.

The sentences should make sense and be grammatically correct. If there are any inconsistencies in use of tense, discuss this with the pupils.

2 Complete each sentence using the **conjunction** in **bold**.

The old man smiled **when** he heard the good news.

The thieves broke in **while** we were away on holiday.

She closed the door **before** Josh could speak.

We played outside **until** the school bell rang.

I was tired **after** I finished the race.

I heard the phone ring **as** I came down the stairs.

Check that the pupils have added a clause [e.g. after I finished the race] rather than a phrase [e.g. after the race], although this will be covered in more detail in Lesson 21.

Check that sentences end with a full stop. There should be no capital letter after the conjunction.

Sentence practice

Write <u>three</u> sentences about what you do when you get home from school. Use <u>three</u> different **conjunctions**.

I get changed when I get home from school. I play games with my brother before I have my tea. Then I watch television until it is bedtime.

These are just examples of sentences that fit the requirements. You could compare the different conjunctions used by the pupils.

Check that the sentences are correctly punctuated with capital letters and full stops.

Lesson 10 Conjunctions to show cause

> Focus   using conjunctions to express cause and effect [e.g. because, as, since, so]
>
> Key terms   conjunction
>
> Focus text   **I was late for school** because **my alarm clock did not go off.**

TEACH

Show the focus text and read it aloud. Discuss what has happened and why. Ask: Which part of the sentence tells us the reason why it happened? [the part starting with the conjunction 'because']

Say that this is rather a boring excuse. Invite the pupils to orally construct sentences giving other reasons [real or imaginary] for being late for school [e.g. I was late for school because … the bus broke down; an elephant was blocking the road]. Ask the pupils to say the complete sentence.

Explain that 'because' is a useful conjunction because it helps us give the cause of an event – the reason why it happened. Explain that there are other conjunctions that we can use to show cause.

Use some of the pupils' earlier suggestions to demonstrate using the conjunctions 'as' and 'since' [e.g. I was late for school <u>as</u> the bus broke down. I was late for school <u>since</u> an elephant was blocking the road.]. Invite the pupils to orally construct some other examples using these conjunctions [e.g. I was late for school <u>as</u> I overslept.].

The pupils will probably notice that 'as' and 'since' can also be used to show time in sentences. Explain that some conjunctions have more than one meaning and use.

Introduce the conjunction 'so'. Explain that if we put the cause or reason *first*, we can use 'so'. It introduces the effect or resulting event [e.g. I overslept <u>so</u> I was late for school.].

EXTEND   Introduce other conjunctions or words used to give reasons [e.g. therefore].

PRACTISE

Pupil book page 13

APPLY

- The pupils use 'because' to show cause and effect when writing explanations.
- Challenge the pupils to use other conjunctions apart from 'because' to give a reason or show a cause. Ask them to highlight the conjunctions they have used.
- Encourage the use of conjunctions when writing in other subject areas [e.g. in science – Bees are important because/as/since …; in history – This was an important event because/as …].
- The pupils write a list of excuses [or a list poem] using conjunctions to explain why an event happened.
- The pupils write a letter from a character in a story, explaining why an event occurred [e.g. I had to sell the cow as we had no money.].

ASSESS

Dictation: My leg was hurting so I went to see the doctor.

Say: Now rewrite the sentence, using the conjunction 'because', 'since' or 'as'.

Answer: e.g. I went to see the doctor because/since/as my leg was hurting.

Pupil book answers

Conjunctions to show cause

Remember

Conjunctions such as 'because', 'as' and 'since' are used to show the cause or reason for an event. They help to tell you <u>why</u>.

I was late for school because <u>my alarm clock did not go off</u>.

Try it

1 Underline the cause or reason for the action or event in each sentence. Circle the **conjunction**.

She stayed in bed all day (because) <u>she was ill</u>.

I left the last sandwich (as) <u>I don't really like cheese</u>.

We had to turn back (since) <u>all the roads were blocked</u>.

School will be closed on Monday (as) <u>it is a holiday</u>.

She went to look in the fridge (because) <u>she felt hungry</u>.

You can go out to play (since) <u>you have finished your work</u>.

<u>He was lost</u> (so) he looked at his map.

2 Complete each sentence by adding a cause or reason next to the **conjunction** in **bold**.

We can't plant the vegetables outside **as** it is much too cold.

The boat will not float **because** it is full of water.

We couldn't cross the bridge **since** it was damaged in the storm.

We went to the pet shop **because** we needed some dog biscuits.

Jack heard footsteps **so** he hid in the cupboard.

I shall wear my wellington boots **as** it is snowing.

Sentence practice

Write a sentence to say why you could not do your homework. Use a **conjunction**.

I could not do my homework as I left my book on the bus.

13

These are just examples of how the sentences might be completed. You could compare the different reasons added by the pupils.

The sentences should make sense and be grammatically correct. Check tense consistency.

Check also that the sentences end with a full stop. There should be no capital letter after the conjunction.

This is just an example of a sentence using a conjunction to introduce the cause. You could compare the different reasons given by the pupils and the conjunctions they have used.

Check that the sentence is correctly punctuated.

29

Revision 1 answers

Focus: forming adjectives using the suffixes –ful and –less

The suffixes should be spelt correctly [e.g. –ful, not –full]. Accept 'fearsome' in the third sentence, but do not accept 'tasty' in the fourth sentence as it does not make sense in the noun phrase.

This page revises elements of word building from **Grammar 1** and **2**, together with the use of grammatical terms. Word building has not yet been covered in this book, so it is important to check that the pupils have retained this knowledge. The focus of each activity is given to help you identify areas where the pupils might need further revision.

Grammar 3

Revision 1

1 Add the missing **suffix** to complete the **adjective** in each noun phrase.

a wise and power<u>ful</u> leader

a faith<u>ful</u> old dog

a brave and fear<u>less</u> explorer

a refreshing but taste<u>less</u> drink

Focus: how the prefix un– changes the meaning of adjectives

Accept any adjective that starts with un– and fits the context. The pupils need to understand that adding un– to an adjective makes it mean the opposite.

2 Complete each sentence with an **adjective** that starts with **un–**.

Katie thought the punishment was <u>unfair</u>.

Dad was annoyed because my bedroom was <u>untidy</u>.

They did not like the <u>unusual</u> smell.

We were <u>unlucky</u> to lose the game.

Focus: verbs and verb endings to show tense

The verbs in the first two sentences must be in the past tense. The verbs in the last two must be in the progressive form [with –ing endings].

Although any verb that makes grammatical sense is acceptable [e.g. looked, looking], this is a good activity for discussing effective choice of verbs.

3 Write a **verb** to complete each sentence. Use the correct **verb form** and check the **tense**.

The king's voice boomed as he <u>stormed</u> into the room.

I lay on the floor and <u>peered</u> under the bed.

Police are <u>searching</u> for the bank robbers.

Flora knew that someone was <u>staring</u> at her.

4 Rewrite each sentence so that each **noun** is a **plural**.

We saw the horse and pony in the stable.
<u>We saw (the) horses and ponies in the stables.</u>

The lorry took the box to the shop.
<u>(The) Lorries took the boxes to the shops.</u>

The teacher took the child to the garden.
<u>The teachers took the children to the gardens.</u>

14

Focus: singular and plural; regular plural noun suffixes –s or –es

The pupils need to recognise the three nouns in the sentence and know how to make them into plurals. The plural nouns should be spelt correctly.

The sentences should be punctuated correctly.

This page revises punctuation introduced in **Grammar 1** and **2** and reinforced in Section 1. The punctuation on this page should now be secure in the pupils' writing. The focus of each activity is given to help identify areas that may need further reinforcement.

Grammar 3

5 Rewrite each sentence using **capital letters** in the correct places.

sir edmund hillary climbed mount everest in may 1953.
Sir Edmund Hillary climbed Mount Everest in May 1953.

You will find moorton primary school on upland road in newtown.
You will find Moorton Primary School on Upland Road in Newtown.

Next friday tom and i will go to Leeds to see Matt.
Next Friday Tom and I will go to Leeds to see Matt.

6 Rewrite the underlined words as a **contraction** using an **apostrophe**.

I <u>have not</u> seen the film yet.   haven't

It <u>does not</u> seem fair.   doesn't

<u>She is</u> late again.   She's

He <u>is not</u> coming.   isn't

<u>It is</u> my birthday today.   It's

7 Here is the start of a story. It is missing **full stops** and **capital letters**. Add them in.

T   S
there was once a frail old woman. she lived all alone with her two
                         T
dogs in a little house. there was never much to eat because the old

woman had no money.

8 Here is part of a thank-you note. Add the missing **sentence punctuation**.

                                      W
Thank you for the birthday present. what a brilliant surprise! I really
                                                   D
wanted a new camera because I broke mine. did you know?

Focus: demarcating sentence boundaries with capital letters, full stops, question marks and exclamation marks

The pupils need to identify sentence boundaries and demarcate them with a capital letter and the correct end punctuation.

Check that no full stop has been added after 'camera' – the pupils need to realise that the sentence continues with 'because'.

Focus: capital letters for proper nouns

You could ask the pupils to explain why these words need capital letters [names of people, places and things].

Focus: using apostrophes in simple contracted forms

Correct spelling and correct placement of the apostrophe is required. [If necessary, remind the pupils that the apostrophe goes in place of the missing letter, and not where the two words join.]

The third and fifth answers should be written with a capital letter.

Focus: demarcating sentence boundaries with capital letters and full stops

The pupils need to demarcate the ends of sentences with a capital letter and full stop. Encourage those who are still struggling to read their writing aloud, listening for sentence breaks.

15

Writing task 1: Analysis sheet

Tick the circles to show amount of evidence found in writing:
1 No evidence
2 Some evidence
3 Clear evidence

Pupil name: _____

Date: _____

Assessing punctuation

The writing sample demonstrates:	Evidence		
sentence boundaries demarcated with capital letters and full stops.	①	②	③
question marks and exclamation marks used appropriately when required.	①	②	③
capital letters used for 'I' and proper nouns.	①	②	③
commas used to separate items in a list [e.g. It was topped with chocolate sprinkles, white marshmallows and a sparkler.].	①	②	③
apostrophes used in contracted forms or for singular possession [e.g. it's delicious; Dad's favourite].	①	②	③

Assessing grammar and sentence structure

The writing sample demonstrates:	Evidence		
grammatically correct sentences.	①	②	③
different sentence types [e.g. statements about the meal; an exclamation – 'What an amazing taste!'].	①	②	③
co-ordinating conjunctions [and, but, or] to join words or clauses [e.g. hot but not too hot].	①	②	③
subordinating conjunctions to show time or cause [e.g. You will love it if you like ice cream. I smelt it before I tasted it.].	①	②	③
correct and consistent use of tense [present or past].	①	②	③
appropriate use of adjectives and adverbs [e.g. golden crust; delicious sauce; I ate it slowly.].	①	②	③
expanded noun phrases to describe and specify [e.g. a juicy burger with cheese on top].	①	②	③

Key target: _____

Writing task 1: Pupil checklist

Name: _____   Date: _____

Reread what you have written to check that it makes sense. Tick the circle if you have correctly used the punctuation or grammar feature in your writing.

Punctuation

- ( ) I have used capital letters at the beginning of sentences.
- ( ) I have used full stops at the end of sentences.
- ( ) I have used a question mark or exclamation mark if it is needed.
- ( ) I have used capital letters for 'I' and any names.
- ( ) I have used commas to separate items in a list.
- ( ) I have used apostrophes when they are needed.

Grammar and sentences

- ( ) I have written in sentences and they make sense.
- ( ) I have used different types of sentence (e.g. statements, exclamations).
- ( ) I have used the conjunctions 'and', 'but', 'or' to make some longer sentences.
- ( ) I have used conjunctions like 'because', 'if', 'when', 'before', 'after', 'while', 'as' to give more information in a sentence.
- ( ) I have used the correct tense in my writing.
- ( ) I have used adjectives (e.g. crunchy, spicy, delicious) and some adverbs (e.g. slowly).
- ( ) I have used longer noun phrases (e.g. a big juicy burger with cheese on top).

Teacher feedback

My key target: _____

_____

Lesson 11 Adverbs to show how

Focus revising 'how' adverbs [those ending –ly and others]

Key terms adverb, suffix, verb, adjective

Focus text She lifted the plate carefully from the side table. The huge jelly wobbled slightly so she carried it really slowly. The guests stood still. They watched anxiously as the maid placed the jelly very gently before the king.

TEACH

Show the focus text. Read it aloud and act out the events described. Read each sentence, discussing which words tell us *how* each action was performed [the highlighted words – the adverbs].

The pupils should be familiar with 'how' adverbs ending with –ly, as these were introduced in **Grammar 2** [e.g. carefully; slowly], but they may notice that some of the highlighted words in the focus text do not end with –ly.

Remind the pupils that adverbs are words that add more detail about the action or verb in a sentence. Adverbs like those in the focus text give extra detail about *how* the action is performed.

Remind the pupils that lots of these 'how' adverbs are formed with the suffix –ly added to an adjective. Ask the pupils if they can suggest any other adverbs like these [e.g. softly; smoothly].

Explain that not all adverbs end with –ly. For example, in the sentence 'The guests stood still.', 'still' is an adverb because it tells us more about *how* the guests stood, but it does not end with –ly. Say other sentences with adverbs that do not end with –ly [e.g. The chefs worked <u>hard</u>. The servants did <u>well</u>.]. Ask the pupils to identify the adverb – the word that tells us more about *how* the action [or verb] was performed.

The pupils may notice that there are two highlighted words in some sentences [really slowly; very gently]. Explain that 'very' and 'really' are adverbs that can be used with other adverbs. They modify the other adverb [e.g. making it stronger].

EXTEND Discuss other adverbs that can be used to modify another adverb [e.g. fairly; quite]. You could explain that these adverbs can also be used with adjectives [e.g. The jelly was very big/really big/quite big.].

PRACTISE

Pupil book page 18

APPLY

* When reading, notice any 'how' adverbs and explore their meanings [e.g. anxiously; cautiously]. Collect and record them for the pupils to use in story writing.
* The pupils use 'how' adverbs in play scripts to show how lines are spoken [e.g. angrily; quietly].
* Encourage the use of adverbs in stories to show a character's feelings [e.g. sadly; happily; crossly].
* Look for 'how' adverbs in different types of writing [e.g. in instructions – gradually, carefully]. Encourage the pupils to collect and use them in similar writing.
* Before writing descriptions, discuss possible adverbs to use [e.g. to describe a storm].

ASSESS

Dictation: The sun seemed to shine <u>brightly</u> in the sky after the darkness of the cave.
Say: Underline the adverb in the sentence.
Check: The sentence punctuation is correct.

Pupil book answers

Adverbs to show how

Remember

Adverbs give extra detail about the **verb** or action in a sentence.
Adverbs can tell you how the action is performed.
Many adverbs end with **–ly**, but some do not.

She carried the jelly slowly. The jelly wobbled
slightly. Everyone stood still.

Try it

1 Underline the **adverb** in each sentence.

Everyone waited <u>nervously</u> for the show to begin.

The play was great and all the children sang <u>well</u>.

Poor Ben tripped and fell <u>awkwardly</u> on the stage.

The actors bowed <u>proudly</u> at the end of the show.

Ms Wilkinson thanked the children for working <u>hard</u>.

The children listened <u>politely</u> to her speech.

2 Rewrite each sentence below, adding a suitable **adverb** to say how the
action happened.

The parrot squawked.   The parrot squawked very loudly.

He shuffled his feet.   He shuffled his feet nervously.

The cat landed on the grass.   The cat landed safely on the grass.

She gripped the rope.   She gripped the rope tightly.

The harvest was gathered.   The harvest was safely gathered.

The boy whispered.   The boy whispered shyly.

Sentence practice

Write <u>two</u> sentences about the start of a snowstorm. Use an **adverb** in
each sentence.

The snow began to fall heavily. The children quickly rushed outside.

18

Check that the pupils
have identified the
adverbs that do not
end with –ly (in the
second and fifth
sentences).

These are just examples
of adverbs the pupils
might choose. The
adverb should fit the
context of the sentence.
In some sentences, the
adverb could be placed
in different positions.
You could compare
the pupils' choices,
discussing why they
were chosen.

Adverbs ending
with –ly should be
spelt correctly unless
the pupils have
chosen particularly
adventurous adverbs.

This is just an example of two possible sentences using
adverbs. Check that the adverbs are spelt correctly.

Lesson 12 Adverbs to show time and place

Focus using adverbs to express time and place

Key terms adverb

Focus text **Mr Magico the magician will appear** soon.
Mr Magico the magician will appear here.
tomorrow   next   shortly   now   later
there   outside   inside   nearby

TEACH

Show the focus text and read aloud the first sentence. Discuss the purpose of the highlighted word. Ask: What extra detail does it give? [when Mr Magico will appear] Read aloud the second sentence. Discuss what the highlighted word tells us this time [where he will appear].

Ask the pupils if they can work out what type of word is highlighted in these sentences [adverbs – they give more detail about the verb].

Explain that as well as telling us how actions are performed, adverbs can also give more detail about *when* and *where* actions are performed. Some of these adverbs end with –ly [e.g. shortly; immediately; presently; eventually; recently], but many do not.

Reveal the adverbs at the bottom of the focus text. Invite the pupils to use these adverbs to construct more sentences about Mr Magico, adding each adverb in turn to the end of the sentence. Identify which adverbs tell us when [tomorrow, next, shortly, now, later] and which ones tell us where [there, outside, inside, nearby].

Introduce some other examples of adverbs that show time [e.g. today; immediately; afterwards; yesterday; first] and ask the pupils to use these in appropriate sentences [e.g. Mr Magico appeared yesterday.].

Discuss how other adverbs can be added to the time adverbs to modify them [e.g. very soon; quite soon; almost immediately; much later].

EXTEND Discuss adverbs that tell us *how often* [e.g. Mr Magico appears often/sometimes/frequently.].

PRACTISE

Pupil book page 19

APPLY

- Encourage the use of adverbs to show time and place when writing stories or accounts with a sequence of events.
- Discuss the use of time and place adverbs in other types of writing [e.g. in instructions – now, next].
- The pupils write posters for events, using adverbs to give details about time and place [e.g. there will be refreshments afterwards; the display will be outside].
- The pupils make lists of time adverbs with similar meanings [e.g. soon, shortly, presently; then, next, afterwards]. They then refer to these when writing, to encourage the use of a range of adverbs to express time.

ASSESS

Dictation: I am at school <u>now</u> but I will be home <u>soon</u>. I am going swimming <u>later</u>.
Say: Underline the three adverbs in these sentences.
Check: The sentence punctuation is correct.

Pupil book answers

Adverbs to show time and place

Remember

Adverbs tell you more about the **verb** or action in a sentence. Some adverbs tell you where or when the action happens.

Mr Magico the magician will appear soon.   (when)
Mr Magico the magician will appear here.   (where)

Try it

1 Underline the **adverb** that says when or where each event happened.

There was a bank raid <u>yesterday</u>.

The police arrived and parked <u>outside</u>.

They cleared the area <u>first</u>.

The police began to search <u>everywhere</u>.

A second police car arrived <u>afterwards</u>.

They found the stolen money <u>nearby</u>.

Point out that the rest of the sentence makes sense without the adverb – the adverb adds more detail to it. You could discuss which adverbs show time [when] and which show place [where].

2 Add an **adverb** from the box to each sentence to say <u>when</u> the action happens. Use each adverb only <u>once</u>.

| soon   today   shortly   now   later   immediately |

The train will arrive ___shortly___.

We went to the library ___today___.

I can play football with you ___later___.

He dealt with the problem ___immediately___.

We are leaving for the station ___now___.

Let's stop for lunch ___soon___.

In some sentences alternative adverbs work just as well [e.g. in the third sentence: 'I can play football with you now.'].

Sentence practice

Write a sentence using **adverbs** to say where <u>and</u> when a talent show will begin.

The talent show will begin here soon.

19

Check that the pupils have used adverbs as instructed rather than phrases such as 'at 4 o'clock'.

Lesson 13 Prepositions to show place

Focus introducing prepositions; using prepositions to express place

Key terms **preposition**, noun, noun phrase, **prepositional phrase**

Focus text The runaway tractor rolled down the hill. It splashed across the stream. It rattled under the bridge. It bashed through the gate. It spluttered into the farmyard and finally stopped on the grass by the duck pond.

TEACH

Show the focus text and read it aloud. Discuss where the runaway tractor went and where its final position was. Underline all the phrases that tell us this [e.g. down the hill; across the stream].

Read the highlighted words at the start of the underlined phrases. Ask the pupils to compose more phrases starting with these words, imagining where else the runaway tractor might have gone to [e.g. down the road; across the field; through the barn; into the stables].

Explain that the highlighted words are called prepositions. A preposition is a word that tells us how one thing relates to another – for example, in terms of position or place [e.g. where the runaway tractor is in relation to the the bridge/the gate/the duck pond].

Look at each of the underlined phrases in the focus text. Explain that each one starts with a preposition, which is then followed by a noun or noun phrase [e.g. the hill; the stream]. Phrases like these, starting with prepositions, are sometimes called prepositional phrases. We can use them to show *where* something is – its position and [if moving] direction.

Replace some of the prepositions in the focus text with their opposites [e.g. up the hill; over the bridge] and discuss how this changes the meaning. Invite the pupils to create more sentences using these or other prepositions [e.g. The runaway tractor rolled over the fields.].

EXTEND Explore more prepositions, discussing words with similar or opposite meanings [e.g. under, beneath, below; inside/outside].

PRACTISE

Pupil book page 20

APPLY

- When writing stories, encourage the use of prepositions to add detail about where events take place [e.g. in the garden; by the shed; under the rose bush].
- When writing descriptions of places or characters, focus on the use of prepositions to add descriptive detail [e.g. The little man stood by the door. He wore a red hat on his head.].
- Look at how prepositions are used to clarify instructions [e.g. bake in a hot oven; leave to cool on a tray]. Ask the pupils to use similar phrases when writing their own instructions.
- The pupils use prepositional phrases to give a guided tour of a real or imaginary place [e.g. Go into the ballroom. Look above the fireplace.].

ASSESS

Dictation: The man was riding on a horse. He stopped by the tall oak tree in the marketplace. He looked over the fence.

Say: Underline the four prepositions in these sentences.

Check: The sentence punctuation is correct.

Pupil book answers

Prepositions to show place

Remember

Prepositions tell you where something is in relation to something else.

The runaway tractor rattled under the bridge.

The tractor stopped on the grass by the duck pond.

Try it

1 Underline the **preposition** or prepositions in each sentence.

The wind blew the woman's hat off her head.

It flew through the air and it landed in a tree.

The woman saw it fall from the branch and drop on to the wall.

Then the hat fell over the wall and landed beside the bins.

The woman ran into the garden and found her hat by a rubbish bag.

2 Choose a **preposition** from the box to complete each sentence. Use each preposition only once.

above	at	beneath	inside	under
across	behind	down	on	up

The goblin lived ____under____ the bridge.

There was a sign ____above____ the shop.

The woman climbed ____up____ the mountain.

Oliver is ____at____ Mary's house.

They sat ____on____ the beach ____beneath____ a palm tree.

He found the treasure ____inside____ the cave ____behind____ a large rock.

She ran ____across____ the road and hurried ____down____ Blake Street.

Other prepositions could be used, particularly words with similar meanings [e.g. under/beneath] or opposites [e.g. up/down]. Compare the pupils' choices, checking that they make sense.

Sentence practice

Write a sentence about where you saw Stefan's dog. Use two prepositions.

We saw Stefan's dog beneath the clock tower in the high street.

20

This is just an example of a sentence using two prepositional phrases.

Check that the sentence is also punctuated correctly, including the use of capital letters for proper nouns and an apostrophe for possession.

Lesson 14 Prepositions to show time

Focus using prepositions to express time

Key terms preposition, noun, noun phrase, prepositional phrase, conjunction

Focus text **The ghost appeared ...**

in **the evening**   on **Monday morning**   after **breakfast**
during **the party**   before **midnight**

TEACH

Show the focus text. Ask the pupils to help you orally construct sentences by adding in turn each of the given phrases to the original sentence [e.g. The ghost appeared in the evening.].

Discuss the purpose or function of these added phrases [they tell us when the ghost appeared]. Look at the highlighted words that start each phrase. Ask the pupils what type of word they are [prepositions]. The pupils should recognise some of the prepositions from the previous lesson [e.g. on; in].

Create other prepositional phrases to add to the sentence by changing the noun or noun phrase that comes after the preposition [e.g. on Saturday evening; after lunch; during the night; before noon].

Explain that the highlighted words are prepositions, but rather than telling us about place or position [where], they tell us about time, or *when* something happened in relation to something else.

Look at each prepositional phrase in the focus text and underline the nouns and noun phrases that follow the preposition [the evening, Monday morning, the party, breakfast, midnight]. Explain that a preposition is followed by a noun or noun phrase. This is important, as the pupils may notice that some of these words can also be used as conjunctions [before, after]. It is a preposition if followed by a noun or noun phrase [e.g. after breakfast], but a conjunction if followed by part of a sentence with a verb [e.g. after we had breakfast]. [Note: This can be confusing but will be covered again in Lesson 21.]

The pupils may also notice that some prepositions can be used to indicate both time *and* place [e.g. <u>on</u> Sunday morning/<u>on</u> the bridge; <u>in</u> the morning/<u>in</u> the doorway].

EXTEND Create sentences using prepositions to show both time and place [e.g. The ghost appeared on Sunday morning by the tall oak tree. Or: On Sunday morning, the ghost appeared by the tall oak tree.].

PRACTISE

Pupil book page 21

APPLY

- When writing stories or accounts, encourage the pupils to use prepositional phrases to show time [e.g. in the evening; during the night; at midnight; by morning], as well as adverbs.
- When reading stories or accounts together, look at different ways of showing time [e.g. adverbs – soon, suddenly; prepositional phrases – in the morning ...; conjunctions – when the prince arrived].
- Encourage the use of prepositional phrases to show time in history [e.g. in the sixteenth century; during his reign].
- The pupils write an account of a day at school, using prepositions to show different times of the day.

ASSESS

Dictation: There was a knock on the door <u>in the middle of the night</u>.
Say: Underline the prepositional phrase used to show time. Then rewrite the sentence using a different time preposition.
Answer: e.g. during the night

Pupil book answers

Prepositions to show time

Remember

Prepositions can also show when an event happened. The preposition is followed by a **noun** or **noun phrase** to make a prepositional phrase.

The ghost appeared after breakfast.

The ghost appeared on Sunday morning.

Try it

1 Add a **preposition** from the box to each sentence to show when the event happens. Use each preposition only once.

> at   before   during   for   in   until

Snow fell ___during___ the night.

They waited ___for___ two hours.

The old man woke up ___at___ dawn.

I will be with you ___in___ a moment.

Mum always goes for a run ___before___ work.

We were best friends ___until___ the argument.

2 Complete the phrase after the **preposition** in **bold** to say when each event takes place.

I must visit Gran **on** Monday.

He will be here **in** a little while.

The clock began to chime **at** four o'clock.

We played football **for** two hours.

You must finish the story **before** lunchtime.

The competition is open **until** the end of March.

Sentence practice

Write a sentence saying when you do P.E. Use at least one preposition.

We do PE after break on Thursday afternoon.

Discuss any sentences where the pupils have used a preposition that shows place rather than time [e.g. Mum always goes for a run at work.].

These are just examples of how the sentences might be completed. Make sure the added phrases say when the event took place, not where.

Check that 'before' and 'until' are followed by nouns or noun phrases rather than by another event [e.g. 'We must finish the story before we go to lunch.' uses 'before' as a conjunction rather than a preposition. This can be confusing, but will be covered in more detail in Lesson 21.].

21

This is an example of a suitable sentence – it uses two prepositions to show time [after, on].

Lesson 15 Inverted commas in direct speech

Focus placing inverted commas [speech marks] around the spoken words in direct speech

Key terms **direct speech, inverted commas [speech marks]**, punctuation, comma

Focus text "My name is Mark 6," said the robot.
"That's a strange name," said Charlie.
"I am programmed to serve you and your family," said Mark 6.
"Cool," said Charlie. "Bring me a glass of milk."

TEACH

Show the focus text. Explain that this is part of a dialogue between two characters in a story. Read it aloud using an appropriate voice for the robot character. Discuss who the characters are and how we can tell who is speaking each time [e.g. it says 'said the robot' and 'said Charlie']. Ask: How can we tell which words are spoken? [the spoken words are inside the speech marks] Underline the spoken words in each line of the focus text. Ask the pupils to read these parts aloud.

Explain that the focus text is an example of direct speech – this is when we write what is said using the actual words spoken. Discuss how the special layout of direct speech makes it clear who is speaking [e.g. a new line is started each time there is a new speaker]. The name of the speaker is added after the spoken words, using the word 'said' or a similar verb [e.g. said Charlie].

Explain that punctuation in direct speech helps make it clear which words are actually spoken. Introduce the term 'inverted commas' [also called 'speech marks']. Circle each set of inverted commas in the focus text. Explain that they go at the start and end of the words actually spoken. The words that are not spoken [e.g. said Charlie] go outside the inverted commas.

Explain that there is another punctuation mark that separates the spoken and non-spoken words in the focus text. Ask the pupils what it is [comma]. Explain that the comma always goes *inside* the inverted commas. [Note: Other rules for punctuating direct speech are introduced in the next lesson, Lesson 16, and in **Grammar 4**. The focus of the current lesson is specifically the correct placement of inverted commas around the spoken words.]

EXTEND Discuss how inverted commas are used in the last line of the focus text where there are two spoken sentences. The unspoken 'said Charlie' is placed between the two spoken parts.

PRACTISE

Pupil book page 22

APPLY

- The pupils take a short extract from a play script and turn it into direct speech, placing inverted commas around the spoken words and adding words to say who is speaking.
- The pupils copy lines spoken by characters in stories into speech bubbles. They then rewrite the same lines as direct speech using inverted commas.
- The pupils use speech bubbles to capture ideas for what two characters might say. They then write the dialogue as direct speech, using inverted commas in place of the speech bubbles.

ASSESS

Dictation: "I'll race you to the fence and back," said Max.
"Wait until I'm ready," said Emma.
Check: A new line is begun for the new speaker. All punctuation is correct.

Pupil book answers

Inverted commas in direct speech

Remember

In **direct speech**, **inverted commas** (or speech marks) are used to show which words are spoken. The inverted commas go at the start and the end of the spoken words.

"My name is Mark 6," said the robot.
"That's a strange name," said Charlie.

Try it

1 Underline the spoken words in each sentence. Then add the missing **inverted commas**.

"I don't like sprouts," muttered Vicky.

"Nonsense, they are good for you," said Mum.

"But they are green and smelly," moaned Vicky.

"They are vegetables," replied Mum. "Of course they are green."

"I'm not going to eat them," insisted Vicky grumpily.

"We will see about that," said Mum firmly.

2 Rewrite these sentences with the **inverted commas** in the correct place.

I shall gobble you up, said the troll.

"I shall gobble you up," said the troll.

That's a lovely idea, said Mrs Haines.

"That's a lovely idea," said Mrs Haines.

I will visit my friend the snake, said the monkey.

"I will visit my friend the snake," said the monkey.

Sentence practice

Write a sentence using **direct speech** to follow the sentence below.

"Where are you going with that basket of delicious cakes?" asked the wolf.

"I'm taking them to my grandma's house," said the little girl.

22

This is just an example of a sentence using correctly punctuated direct speech.

Check the use of apostrophes if shortened forms or apostrophes for possession are included.

If the pupils struggle to identify the spoken words, ask them to read the dialogue aloud so they can hear the different parts of the sentence.

Check that the pupils have included the comma within the inverted commas. Remind them to look at the examples if they are not sure. [Note: The next lesson, Lesson 16, will focus on end punctuation within inverted commas.]

Check that the pupils have included the comma at the end of the spoken words and placed it within the inverted commas.

The pupils may find that it helps to first underline the spoken words in the given sentence. This shows where the inverted commas need to go.

Lesson 16 Punctuation in direct speech

Focus using capital letters, end punctuation and inverted commas in direct speech

Key terms direct speech, inverted commas [speech marks], capital letter, comma, question mark, exclamation mark, full stop, punctuation

Focus text **What do we have here then? growled Captain Jack.**
They be stowaways, replied Pirate Bill.
Stowaways! roared Captain Jack.
Yes, Captain. Shall I make them walk the plank? Pirate Pete asked eagerly.

TEACH

Show the focus text. Explain that it is an extract of direct speech taken from a story. Read it aloud using appropriate voices for the pirates. Discuss what is missing [inverted commas or speech marks] and ask why they are necessary [to make it clear which words are actually spoken].

Ask the pupils to help you add the inverted commas. Read each line, discussing which words are spoken. Use a coloured pen to add inverted commas at the start and end of the spoken words.

As you add the inverted commas, discuss the punctuation at the end of the spoken words. Point out that it is not always a comma. Sometimes a question mark or an exclamation mark is used instead. Discuss why [e.g. because it is a question; to show that it is shouted]. Explain that this end punctuation always goes *inside* the inverted commas because it belongs to the spoken words.

Once the inverted commas have been added, discuss when capital letters are used in the focus text [e.g. the first letter of the direct speech; characters' names; a new sentence within the inverted commas]. Explain that the part following the spoken words [e.g. growled ...; replied ...] does *not* begin with a capital letter even after a question mark or exclamation mark – unless it is a name [e.g. Pirate Pete asked].

EXTEND Discuss other verbs that could be used in place of 'said' [e.g. snarled; shouted] or other adverbs that could be added to say *how* words are spoken [e.g. growled angrily].

PRACTISE

Pupil book page 23

APPLY

- Orally rehearse a conversation between two characters that involves using questions and answers [e.g. one character is lost and the other is helping them]. Then ask the pupils to write the dialogue as direct speech using the correct punctuation.
- The pupils write exclamations or questions spoken by characters in familiar stories as direct speech [e.g. "What a beautiful dress!" sighed Cinderella. "Who lost this glass slipper?" asked the prince.].
- When writing direct speech, discuss whether an exclamation mark might be needed. Collect suitable verbs to follow exclamations [e.g. bellowed; exclaimed; cried; shouted; yelled; screamed].
- When writing stories, choose a part where the story can be told through an exchange of questions and answers. Orally rehearse and then ask the pupils to write it as direct speech.

ASSESS

Dictation: "Will you help me carry these watermelons?" asked the farmer.
"I'm much too busy," said the first man.
"Go away!" shouted the second man.
Check: The inverted commas, capital letters and other punctuation marks are correct.

Pupil book answers

Schofield & Sims **Grammar and Punctuation**   Grammar 3

Punctuation in direct speech

Remember

In **direct speech**, you usually put a **comma** at the end of the spoken words. Sometimes you need to use a question mark or exclamation mark instead. This end punctuation always goes inside the **inverted commas**.

"Shall I make them walk the plank?" asked Pirate Pete.

Try it

1 Add the **inverted commas** in the correct place.

"Can you show me a magic trick?" asked George.

"Don't make a noise," warned Riham.

"How clever of me!" laughed the old lady.

"The journey will take many days," explained the captain of the ship.

"Will someone fetch me a drink of water?" the old man asked.

"Go away!" yelled Sam.

2 Rewrite each sentence adding **inverted commas** and the missing end **punctuation**.

Are you feeling better asked the doctor.

 "Are you feeling better?" asked the doctor.

What beautiful colours exclaimed Jude.

 "What beautiful colours!" exclaimed Jude.

Empty your pockets demanded the wizard.

 "Empty your pockets," demanded the wizard.

Sentence practice

Alfie asks his mum if he can go to Zainab's party. Write his question and her answer as **direct speech**, using the correct **punctuation**.

 "Can I go to Zainab's party?" pleaded Alfie.

 "When is it?" asked his mum.

23

Check that the end punctuation is included within the inverted commas.

Check the position of the inverted commas, making sure the end punctuation is included within them.

Check that a capital letter is used at the start of the direct speech and for names, but there should be no capital letter for the verbs that follow the spoken words.

Check that the complete sentence ends with a full stop.

This is just an example. Mum's reply may not be a question [e.g. "Of course you can," said his mum.].

Check both sentences are correctly punctuated, with the correct placement of inverted commas and end punctuation [question mark, comma] within the inverted commas. Check also that capital letters and full stops are used appropriately [e.g. a capital letter for the first word in the inverted commas; no capital letter for 'said' or similar verbs].

Lesson 17 Verbs: past tense

Focus revising the past tense form of verbs [simple and progressive]

Key terms verb, tense, past tense, present tense, **progressive form**

Focus text **When we arrive at the circus, we collect our tickets. We go into the Big Top and find our seats. Music is playing and two clowns are fooling around. It is really noisy and I am very excited.**

TEACH

Show the focus text and read it aloud. Discuss the events [what they do, what they see and hear].

Then discuss what tense is used and how we can tell [e.g. present tense – from looking at the verbs]. Explain that normally an account of an event like this would be in the past tense. Ask the pupils to help you change the verbs in the focus text into the past tense. Read each sentence, discussing the verbs and writing them in the past tense [e.g. arrived; went; found; was playing].

Use the activity to revise the simple past tense and the past progressive form of verbs. For example:

- The first sentence shows regular simple past tense verbs, formed using –ed endings [e.g. arrive/arrived].
- The second sentence shows irregular simple past tense verbs [go/went, find/found].
- The third sentence shows the progressive [or –ing] form of verbs, formed with 'was'/'were' in the past tense ['is'/'are'/'am' in the present tense]. Discuss why the progressive form is used in this particular sentence [because these events are/were in progress for some time].
- The fourth sentence shows that verbs are not always 'doing words'. Verbs can be 'being words', used to express a state of being. The verb 'to be' has many different forms, and changes depending on the subject, or who the sentence is about [e.g. I am/was; she is/was; they are/were].

Remind the pupils that it is important to keep to the same tense. Say some more sentences about the visit to the circus using verbs in the present tense [e.g. We see the ringmaster and everyone cheers. The clowns are dancing and people are laughing.]. Ask the pupils to say them in the past tense.

EXTEND Explore the past tense of some irregular verbs [e.g. buy/bought; creep/crept].

PRACTISE

Pupil book page 24

APPLY

- When writing accounts, encourage the use of the progressive form as well as the simple past tense.
- The pupils write the opening sentence to a story using a progressive form [e.g. Joe was waiting for his dad.].
- The pupils write sentences for stories where actions in progress are interrupted by something exciting [e.g. We were walking down the road when a spaceship landed right in front of us.].
- Discuss the use of the past tense when writing about events in history.
- The pupils write sentences showing a change of tense [e.g. Yesterday it was ... but today it is ...].
- Remind the pupils to check the use of tense in their writing, especially regarding irregular verbs and maintaining the same tense.

ASSESS

Dictation: Dan was working in the garden when he heard a noise. He looked behind the shed and saw a baby dragon.
Say: Write a sentence using a progressive [or –ing] verb to say what the baby dragon was doing.
Answer: e.g. The baby dragon was crying.

Pupil book answers

Verbs: past tense

Remember

To write a **verb** in the **past tense**, you often add **–ed** to the present tense verb. However, some verbs do not follow this pattern.

We collect our tickets.   We collected our tickets.
We find our seats.   We found our seats.

In the past tense, the **progressive** or **–ing form** of verbs uses the words '**was**' and '**were**'.

Music is playing.   Music was playing.

Try it

1 Write the underlined **verbs** in the **past tense**.

She <u>writes</u> a letter and then she <u>posts</u> it.	wrote	posted
The earth <u>shakes</u> when the giant <u>jumps</u>.	shook	jumped
I <u>carry</u> on until I <u>come</u> to a crossroads.	carried	came
Dad <u>cooks</u> some porridge and we <u>eat</u> it.	cooked	ate
We <u>drag</u> the rubbish outside and <u>throw</u> it away.	dragged	threw

> These sentences contain both regular and irregular verbs.
>
> Check that the past tense verbs with –ed are spelt correctly [e.g. carried, dragged]. Revise the spelling patterns for adding –ed if necessary.

2 Write each sentence in the **past tense**, using the **progressive** or **–ing form** of the verb.

Rapunzel washed her hair. Rapunzel was washing her hair.

The young man strolled along. The young man was strolling along.

The queen counted her money. The queen was counting her money.

I found my homework difficult. I was finding my homework difficult.

The dog ate the cake. The dog was eating the cake.

She pointed at something. She was pointing at something.

> Check that the pupils have used the correct progressive forms in the past tense.

Sentence practice

Write a sentence using the **verbs** 'meet' and 'speak' in the **past tense**.

I met a funny little man and he spoke to me.

24

Lesson 18 Verbs: perfect form

Focus introducing the present perfect form of verbs in contrast to the simple past tense

Key terms verb, tense, past tense, present tense, **perfect form**

Focus text Hi! We are camping in Devon. It has rained every day. Our tent has started to leak. So far, we have tried walking in the rain and have gone swimming in the rain. It has been a miserable holiday.

TEACH

Show the focus text. Explain that it is a postcard from someone on holiday. Read it aloud and discuss the situation [e.g. Why has it been a miserable holiday?].

Discuss whether the postcard refers to events in the past or the present [e.g. the first sentence is in the present tense but then the writer refers to things that have happened in the past, earlier in the week]. Read each sentence, stressing the highlighted verbs. Ask the pupils what they notice about these verbs [e.g. there is an extra verb, 'has' or 'have', before the main past tense verbs].

Explain that the highlighted verbs are examples of verbs in the perfect form. The perfect form is used to talk about events or experiences in the past, but it is different from the simple past tense. Recount the events in the focus text using the simple past tense, as if the writer was back home [e.g. Last week, we went camping. It rained every day. Our tent started to leak. We tried walking in the rain and went swimming …]. Explain that in this version the events happened and were completed in the past.

Explain that we use the perfect form when an event began in the past but is still in progress or still has consequences now [e.g. it has rained every day – it is still raining now; our tent has started to leak – it is still leaking so they are getting wet].

Use the highlighted verbs in the focus text to discuss how the perfect tense is formed [e.g. using the extra 'helper' verb 'has' with it/he/she, or 'have' with I/you/we/they]. Explain that the main verb is often the same as the simple past tense verb [e.g. rained; started] but that some verbs use a special form with have/has [e.g. we have gone; it has been].

[Note: This lesson focuses on present perfect forms; the past perfect form is introduced in **Grammar 5**. At this stage, only the term 'perfect form' is used in the pupil book.]

EXTEND Explore other irregular perfect verb forms [e.g. I took lots of photos – I have taken lots of photos]. [Note: Irregular forms are covered in more detail in **Grammar 4**.]

PRACTISE

Pupil book page 25

APPLY

- The pupils use perfect forms to write a letter or diary entry referring to some prior events.
- Discuss the use of perfect verb forms in news reports [e.g. Police have arrested a man.].
- In other subject areas, the pupils use perfect forms to explain the results of events/what has happened [e.g. in science – the roots have taken up the water…].

ASSESS

Dictation: It has poured down all day. I tidied my room. I finished my jigsaw.
Say: Underline the perfect form of a verb. Then change the other verbs into perfect forms.
Answer: have tidied; have finished

Pupil book answers

Verbs: perfect form

Remember

You can use the **perfect form** of **verbs** to write about things that have happened in the past and are still happening now. To do this you put the 'helper' verb '**has**' or '**have**' before the main verb.

It has <u>rained</u> all week.   I have <u>played</u> games.
Dad has <u>finished</u> his book. We have <u>been</u> to a museum.

You could discuss how these sentences are different from the simple past tense where all the events were completed in the past [e.g. I packed my suitcase. Mum planned the route. We <u>were</u> ready to go.].

Try it

1 Add '**has**' or '**have**' to complete these sentences, which all use the perfect form of the verb.

I ___have___ packed my suitcase.

We ___have___ listened to the weather forecast.

Mum ___has___ planned the route.

Dad ___has___ found the deckchairs and the surfboards.

My brother Aiden ___has___ watered the plants.

We ___have___ made a picnic. Now we are ready to go!

2 Rewrite each sentence using the **perfect form** of the **verb**.

They waited for two hours.	They have waited for two hours.
We painted the front door.	We have painted the front door.
She washed her hands.	She has washed her hands.
He ate all the chocolate cake.	He has eaten all the chocolate cake.
I saw Kelly today.	I have seen Kelly today.

You could discuss how using the perfect form draws attention to the consequences of the action [e.g. She has washed her hands – so now they are clean.].

Check that the pupils have used the correct verb form in the last two questions. Introduce these words if they are not familiar with them. [Note: Irregular verbs will be covered in more detail in **Grammar 4**.]

Sentence practice

Write <u>three</u> sentences about things you have done today, using the **perfect form** of the **verbs**.

So far today, I have chatted to my friends. We have played football in the playground. I have read a book with my friend Billy.

25

These are just examples of sentences using perfect verb forms. The pupils may have used irregular forms [e.g. I have eaten my breakfast.]. If so, check that these are correct.

Lesson 19 Nouns with suffixes

> Focus forming nouns using suffixes [e.g. –ment, –ness, –er, –ship, –ation]
>
> Key terms noun, suffix, compound noun, noun phrase, verb, adjective
>
> Focus text **The new** striker **was a** sensation. **Playing his first** game **in the** championship, **he showed incredible** bravery **and a** willingness **to run. A slick** movement **helped him get past the** goalkeeper **to score the** winner.

TEACH

Show the focus text and read it aloud. Discuss what sort of text it might be taken from [e.g. a sports report from a newspaper]. Discuss which words or phrases suggest this, and underline distinctive noun phrases [e.g. the new striker; a sensation; the championship].

Ask the pupils what type of word is highlighted [nouns – they name things]. Not all of these words are obvious nouns, so point out that words like 'sensation', 'willingness' and 'movement' are used with the words 'a' or 'the', which helps to identify them as nouns.

Ask the pupils if they notice anything special about many of these nouns [they have suffixes]. Challenge them to find the compound noun [goalkeeper] and the noun with no suffix [game].

Remind the pupils that suffixes are added to the end of words to make new words. Many nouns are made this way. Look at the nouns in the focus text and identify the original words and the suffixes. Circle the suffixes –er, –ation, –ship, –ery, –ness, –ment.

Discuss how the suffixes change the words. For example, –er is added to a verb to make a person or thing that does something [e.g. a striker strikes the ball; the winner wins the game]. The suffixes –ment and –ation are other examples of suffixes added to verbs to form nouns [e.g. a movement is a thing that happens when something moves].

Remind the pupils that not all nouns are things that we can see or touch or sense. Some nouns name things such as qualities [e.g. bravery; willingness]. Explain that these words are formed by adding suffixes such as –ness to adjectives [e.g. adjective – he is <u>willing</u>; noun – he shows a <u>willingness</u>].

EXTEND Discuss other suffixes that form nouns [e.g. stupidity; kingdom, wisdom; artist].

PRACTISE

Pupil book page 26

APPLY

- When reading different texts, look for words with these suffixes. Build up lists to display in the classroom and encourage the pupils to use them when speaking or writing.
- When talking or writing about the qualities or feelings of characters, challenge the pupils to use sentence stems with nouns ending –ness or –ery [e.g. The weakness of this character is …; You can see her bravery when …].
- Identify nouns with suffixes in other subject areas [e.g. in geography – settlement, building, locality, environment; in history – crime and punishment, entertainment].

ASSESS

Dictation: He showed no <u>nervousness</u> before the <u>examination</u>.
Say: Underline the nouns with suffixes.

Pupil book answers

Nouns with suffixes

Remember

A **suffix** is a group of letters added to the end of a word to make a new word. Some **nouns** are formed by adding a suffix to a word.

striker   champion**ship**   willing**ness**   move**ment**

Try it

1 Add a **suffix** from the box to make each word into a new **noun**.

−er −ation −ship −ness −ment −ing

defend	defender	shred	shredder
pay	payment	punish	punishment
friend	friendship	member	membership
invite	invitation	tempt	temptation
weak	weakness	foolish	foolishness
warn	warning	paint	painting

Check that the nouns are spelt correctly, including those that require a change of spelling [e.g. invitation; shredder]. Ensure that the pupils have formed nouns [e.g. punishment not punishing; shredder not shredding]. If necessary, remind them that they can check that the words are nouns by using them with 'a' or 'the' [e.g. a punishment; the shredder].

2 Use a **suffix** to complete each **noun** in these sentences.

The soft ness   of the pillow made Jo forget about her tired ness   .

The report er   said the show was great entertain ment   .

The juggle r   dropped the hoops, to everyone's amuse ment   .

The settle ment   was made up of six build ings   .

Morgan's one weak ness   is his forgetful ness   .

The work er   and the manage ment   came to an agree ment   .

Accept other nouns that make sense.

Sentence practice

Add a **suffix** to the word 'excite' to make a **noun**. Write a sentence using the new word.

Ava was full of excitement about her birthday sleepover.

This is an example of a sentence using the noun 'excitement' in a suitable context. The word should be spelt correctly.

Lesson 20 Nouns with prefixes

Focus   forming nouns using prefixes [e.g. super–, inter–, auto–]

Key terms **prefix**, noun

Focus text **When we went shopping, we didn't expect to see a** superstar **signing** autographs **in the** supermarket. **She was giving** interviews **about her new** autobiography.

TEACH

Show the focus text and read it aloud. Discuss the events [e.g. Where did they go? Who did they see? What was she doing?]. In answering these questions, the pupils will refer to the highlighted nouns. Ensure that they understand what these words mean [e.g. discuss the purpose of an autobiography].

Ask the pupils what type of word is highlighted [nouns – they name things]. Discuss which nouns begin in the same way as each other [supermarket, superstar; autograph, autobiography].

Explain that the highlighted nouns all begin with a prefix. A prefix is a group of letters added to the start of a word to turn it into another word. The pupils should already be familiar with the prefix un–, which we add to verbs and adjectives to create opposites or reversals [e.g. usual/unusual; do/undo].

Explain that prefixes are sometimes added to words to form nouns. Look at each noun in the focus text and identify the prefix and the original word. Circle the prefixes [super–, auto–, inter–].

Ask the pupils to think of other nouns with the prefix super– [e.g. superhero; Superman; superstore; superbike]. Discuss what the prefix super– means in words like these [e.g. above; more than; bigger/ better than usual]. Discuss the other prefixes from the focus text and their meanings [e.g. auto– means 'self' or 'own'; inter– means 'between']. Together, think of some other prefixes and discuss their meanings [e.g. anti– means 'against'; de– means 'not'; re– means 'again']. Ask the pupils to use dictionaries to find examples of nouns with these prefixes.

EXTEND Introduce other prefixes used in the formation of nouns [e.g. tri– in tricycle; bi– in bicycle; micro– in microchip; oct– in octopus].

PRACTISE

Pupil book page 27

APPLY

- The pupils use dictionaries to find other examples of nouns with the prefixes covered in this lesson. Explain that the number of nouns is growing all the time [e.g. superhighway; interface].
- The pupils look for examples of words with prefixes in adverts [e.g. anti-dandruff shampoo]. They then write their own adverts for a new super-product [e.g. anti-gravity boots].
- The pupils invent their own nouns using the prefixes [e.g. superbridge]. They then write definitions or draw pictures to illustrate what they would be.
- In other curriculum areas, look for words with these or other prefixes [e.g. in maths – subtraction, triangle, semi-circle, anti-clockwise; in computing – internet, interface, autocorrect, microchip].

ASSESS

Dictation: Would you like to do an <u>inter</u>view with <u>Super</u>man in a <u>sub</u>marine?
Say: Underline any prefixes at the beginning of the nouns.
Check: All punctuation is correct, including the capital letter for a name.

Pupil book answers

Nouns with prefixes

Remember

A **prefix** is a group of letters added to the start of a word to make a new word. Some **nouns** are formed by adding a prefix to a word.

supermarket interview

Try it

1 Add a **prefix** from the box to make each word into a new **noun**.

inter– super– sub– anti– auto– over–

sub heading   _inter_ net
inter viewer   _auto_ mobile
auto graph   _super_ star
super woman   _sub_ way
over coat   _auto_ pilot
anti septic   _over_ time

If necessary, help the pupils to use a dictionary to find the words starting with these prefixes [e.g. anti– and auto–], or to check the words they have made.

2 Complete each noun by adding the missing **prefix**.

inter– super– sub– anti– auto– over– re–

When we went to the theatre we had an ice cream in the _inter_ val.

Spiderman is a _super_ hero because he has _super_ powers.

The _sub_ marine sank down to the ocean floor.

After you wash your hands, _re_ apply the _anti_ bacterial cream.

I read Nelson Mandela's _auto_ biography.

The painter put on his _over_ alls before he started to paint the ceiling.

Sentence practice

Write a sentence to explain the meaning of the **noun** 'superstore'.

A superstore is a very large shop that sells lots of different things.

27

The noun should be written as one word with no space.

Revision 2 answers

Focus: 'how' adverbs formed using –ly suffix

These are just examples of suitable adverbs that fit the context of the sentence. Adverbs with the suffix –ly should be spelt correctly.

Focus: expressing time using conjunctions

Accept alternative conjunctions that make grammatical sense in the context of the sentence [e.g. while/as].

If the pupils make inappropriate choices, remind them to think about the meaning. They could orally rehearse sentences first, trying out different conjunctions to see which makes sense.

Focus: use of 'a' or 'an'

Also accept answers that refer to it being easier to say, but *not* answers that just refer to it not sounding right, with no further explanation.

This page revises terms and word classes from the end of **Grammar 2** and Section 1 of this book. The focus of each activity is given to help you identify areas where the pupils might need further revision.

Revision 2

1 Rewrite each sentence, adding a suitable **adverb** to show how the action is peformed.

"Come here!" Mum shouted.
  "Come here!" Mum shouted angrily.

Tears trickled down his face.
  Tears trickled slowly down his face.

The children ran into the playground.
  The children ran happily into the playground.

2 Add a <u>different</u> time **conjunction** to complete each sentence.

The boy hurried home ____when____ he saw it was getting dark.

A fox appeared ____while____ the rabbit was dozing in the sun.

The children played on the swings ____until____ it was time for tea.

I always brush my teeth ____before____ I go to school.

3 Why is the word '**an**' used in the sentence below?

Do you want a strawberry tart or <u>an</u> ice cream?
  Because 'ice cream' starts with a vowel
  sound.

4 Rewrite each sentence with **proper nouns** in place of the underlined nouns and noun phrases.

<u>The man</u> went to <u>the station</u> to get a ticket to <u>town</u>.
  Lee went to Barton station to get a ticket to Kirkby.

<u>The boy</u> invited everyone to the disco at <u>his school</u>.
  Hassan invited everyone to the disco at Acorn Wood School.

<u>The twins</u> went to <u>the theme park</u>.
  Freya and Faye went to Alton Towers.

28

Focus: proper nouns; use of capital letters for proper nouns

If necessary, remind the pupils that a proper noun is a name.

These are just suggestions. The pupils will make their own choices of names. Check that all proper nouns begin with capital letters.

This page revises work on sentences covered in Section 1. The focus of each activity is given to help you identify areas where the pupils might need further revision.

Schofield & Sims **Grammar and Punctuation**   Grammar 3

5 Complete each sentence by giving a reason. Use a <u>different</u> **conjunction** for each one.

I wouldn't want a dragon for a pet because they are dangerous.

I would rather have a dog as you can take them for walks.

6 Add **adjectives** or descriptive phrases to make these nouns into longer **noun phrases**.

the bin   the dirty, smelly bin

the lion   the angry lion with a poorly paw

the suitcase   the battered old suitcase with a broken handle

the table   the big round table in the dining room

7 *Mum walks into the kitchen. Jake has dropped a cheesecake on the floor. It has made a mess.*

Write an **exclamation** Mum might say.

 What a mess!

Write a **question** Mum might ask.

 How did you manage that?

Write a **command** Mum might say.

 Get the dustpan and brush.

8 Write <u>three</u> descriptive sentences about a boat in a storm. Use **adjectives**, **adverbs**, **prepositions** and **conjunctions** to add detail.

 The sea was calm when the little boat set sail. Soon the wind grew stronger and the waves grew bigger. The little boat began to sway and tip in the stormy sea.

Focus: constructing and punctuating sentences

This is just an example of three possible sentences, including some descriptive detail and use of conjunctions and prepositions.

The sentences must be demarcated with capital letters and full stops. If not, ask the pupils to read them aloud, listening for the sentence breaks and putting in the punctuation.

29

Focus: using conjunctions to give reasons

These are examples of appropriate sentences. Other conjunctions could be used [e.g. since].

Focus: nouns and noun phrases modified by adjectives and added detail

These are examples of suitable phrases expanded before and after the noun. Compare the pupils' choice of adjectives.

Focus: writing and punctuating different types of sentence – question, exclamation, command

These are just examples of appropriate sentences with the correct punctuation. The pupils may use inverted commas to show the words are spoken but this is not the focus of the question.

[Note: In the KS2 English grammar and punctuation test, an exclamation is required to start with 'What' or 'How'.]

Writing task 2: Analysis sheet

Tick the circles to show amount of evidence found in writing:
1 No evidence
2 Some evidence
3 Clear evidence

Pupil name: _____

Date: _____

Assessing punctuation

The writing sample demonstrates:	Evidence		
sentence boundaries demarcated with capital letters and full stops.	①	②	③
question marks and exclamation marks used appropriately when required.	①	②	③
capital letters used for 'I' and proper nouns.	①	②	③
commas used to separate items in a list [e.g. We saw fields, hedges and farms.].	①	②	③
apostrophes used in contracted forms or for singular possession [e.g. We went in Dad's car.].	①	②	③
inverted commas used to indicate direct speech [e.g. "We're off!" we all shouted.].	①	②	③

Assessing grammar and sentence structure

The writing sample demonstrates:	Evidence		
grammatically correct sentences.	①	②	③
different sentence types [e.g. Have you ever been to ...? What a brilliant place!].	①	②	③
co-ordinating conjunctions [and, but, or] to join words or clauses.	①	②	③
subordinating conjunctions to show time or cause [e.g. I was excited when ...; I was interested because ...].	①	②	③
correct and consistent use of past tense, including progressive and perfect forms.	①	②	③
adverbs and prepositions to add detail about where, when, how [e.g. through the window; in the morning; suddenly].	①	②	③
adjectives and expanded noun phrases to add detail [e.g. a little country lane with no houses].	①	②	③

Key target: _____

Writing task 2: Pupil checklist

Name: _____   Date: _____

Reread what you have written to check that it makes sense. Tick the circle if you have correctly used the punctuation or grammar feature in your writing.

Punctuation

- ( ) I have used capital letters at the beginning of sentences.
- ( ) I have used full stops at the end of sentences.
- ( ) I have used a question mark or exclamation mark if it is needed.
- ( ) I have used capital letters for 'I' and any names.
- ( ) I have used commas to separate items in a list.
- ( ) I have used apostrophes when they are needed.
- ( ) I have used inverted commas for any direct speech.

Grammar and sentences

- ( ) I have written in sentences and they make sense.
- ( ) I have used different types of sentence (e.g. statements, questions, exclamations, commands).
- ( ) I have used the conjunctions 'and', 'but', 'or' to make some longer sentences.
- ( ) I have used conjunctions to say when or why (e.g. when, before, after, while, as, because, since).
- ( ) I have used the correct tense in my writing.
- ( ) I have used adverbs and prepositions to say where, when or how (e.g. through the window, in the morning, suddenly).
- ( ) I have used adjectives and longer noun phrases to give detail (e.g. a little country lane with no houses).

Teacher feedback

My key target: _____

_____

Lesson 21 Clauses and phrases

Focus using the terms 'clause' and 'phrase' in relation to forming sentences

Key terms sentence, word, **phrase**, **clause**, **main clause**, verb, noun phrase, prepositional phrase

Focus text Ideas 1: a man was walking   snow began to fall
                         he heard an owl

            Ideas 2: in a thin mist   along the dark road   in the woods
                         one cold night

TEACH

Show the focus text. Read 'Ideas 1' aloud. Discuss whether they sound like complete sentences [yes, they just need a capital letter and full stop]. Read 'Ideas 2'. Do they sound like complete sentences? [no, they are the sort of phrases that we use in sentences to give more detail about events]

Invite the pupils to use phrases from Ideas 2 to expand on Ideas 1. Encourage them to orally rehearse sentences, trying out different constructions [e.g. One cold night, a man was walking along the dark road. Snow began to fall in a thin mist. He heard an owl in the woods nearby.].

Explain that sentences are made up of words, phrases and clauses. Remind the pupils that a phrase is a group of words that go together. They should already be familiar with noun phrases [e.g. one cold night] and prepositional phrases [e.g. in the woods] like those in the focus text. A phrase is not a complete sentence – it does not tell the reader something like a sentence does.

Introduce the term 'clause'. Explain that a clause is special because it contains a verb or a verb with a 'helper' verb. Look at Ideas 1. These clauses have a subject [man, snow, he] and a verb. Each idea makes sense and tells the reader something. It sounds like a sentence and with the correct punctuation it would be a one-clause sentence. These are main clauses. We can add phrases like those in Ideas 2 to a one-clause sentence to make it longer or more detailed.

EXTEND Discuss how to use the conjunctions 'and' or 'but' to join two sentences or two main clauses together to make one longer sentence [e.g. A man was walking and he heard an owl.].

PRACTISE

Pupil book page 32

APPLY

- Encourage oral rehearsal of sentences before they are written down. Remind the pupils to improve sentences by adding phrases to give more detail about the main clause.
- Challenge the pupils to trim back sentences, deleting all descriptive words, adverbs and prepositional phrases, to leave just the main clause [e.g. he disappeared].
- The pupils write a paragraph using some longer sentences with added words and phrases and one or two short sentences with just one main clause.

ASSESS

Dictation: The man sat on a rock beside the river. It was warm in the sunshine.
Say: Underline the main clause in each sentence without any of the added phrases.

Pupil book answers

Clauses and phrases

Remember

A **phrase** is a group of words that go together but do **not** make a complete sentence.

in the woods   one cold night

A **clause** is a group of words that go together and include a **verb**. Some clauses are complete sentences – they make sense on their own. These are **main clauses**.

snow began to fall   he heard an owl

Try it

1 Tick the correct box to show whether each group of words is a **clause** or a **phrase**.

	clause	phrase
in the classroom		✓
the room was quiet	✓	
the bell rang	✓	
the boy with a cheeky grin		✓
Aruna rushed in	✓	

Remind the pupils that a clause has a verb, tells the reader something, and makes sense on its own.

2 Add a **clause** to these **phrases** to complete each sentence.

_____The lorry stopped_____ at the traffic lights in Hope Street.

_____Mum sat down_____ on a comfortable chair by the fireplace.

_____We were lost_____ in a maze of tunnels.

_____The boy ran_____ down the corridor.

_____The cat peered at him_____ with sharp green eyes.

These are just examples of clauses that complete the sentences. You could compare the pupils' answers, discussing the verbs or the subject of the sentence.

Check that the sentences begin with capital letters.

Sentence practice

Write a sentence about a juggler, using **one** **clause** and **one** added **phrase**.

32

_____The juggler dropped the balls on the floor._____

This is just an example of a sentence that meets the requirements.

Lesson 22 **Subordinate clauses**

Focus using the terms 'main clause' and 'subordinate clause' in relation to sentences

Key terms clause, main clause, **subordinate clause**, sentence, conjunction

Focus text Archie screamed.
Archie screamed because he hated spiders.
Archie screamed when the lights went off.
Archie screamed as the rollercoaster plunged down.
Archie screamed although no-one could hear him.

TEACH

Show the first sentence of the focus text. Explain that this is a sentence with one main clause. Reveal and read the other sentences, discussing what information is added [why he screamed, when he screamed, why it was useless]. Ask: How is it added? [using the highlighted conjunctions]. Discuss the new conjunction 'although', which is used to introduce a contrast or something unexpected.

Discuss how many clauses there are in each sentence [two: 'Archie screamed' and another clause starting with the conjunction. They are clauses because they include a verb and tell us something.].

Explain that there are two types of clause: main clauses and subordinate clauses. A main clause makes sense on its own and can stand alone as a sentence [e.g. Archie screamed.].

A subordinate clause is one added to a main clause to give more detail. A conjunction such as 'because' or 'when' is often used at the start of a subordinate clause. These are called subordinating conjunctions. [Note: The pupils do not need to know this term yet – it is introduced in **Grammar 4** – but you can introduce it here if you wish.] Read each sentence in the focus text, underlining the subordinate clause – the part that begins with the conjunction [e.g. because he hated spiders; when the lights went off].

[Note: Other types of subordinate clause are introduced in **Grammar 5**.]

Explain that 'subordinate' means 'less important'. A subordinate clause is less important because it only adds more to a main clause – it does not make sense on its own. So, for example, 'because he hated spiders' does not make sense without the main clause – we do not know who or what it is referring to.

Invite the pupils to suggest other subordinate clauses for the sentence 'Archie screamed', using other subordinating conjunctions [e.g. while; before].

EXTEND Explain that although the subordinate clause is often added *after* the main clause as in the focus text, it can be added before it [e.g. When the lights went off, Archie screamed.]. [Note: This is covered in **Grammar 4**.]

PRACTISE

Pupil book page 33

APPLY

- Encourage the pupils to use sentences with subordinate clauses in their writing, using a variety of conjunctions.
- Remind the pupils to orally rehearse sentences with subordinate clauses before writing them.
- When they are revising their writing, ask the pupils to underline any subordinate clauses they have used.

ASSESS

Dictation: The man whistled as he strolled along the path. He did not stop until he came to a gate.
Say: Underline the subordinate clause in each sentence.

60

Pupil book answers

Subordinate clauses

Remember

You can use a **conjunction** to add another clause to a **main clause**.

Archie screamed <u>because</u> he hated spiders.

This extra clause is a **subordinate clause**. A subordinate clause usually starts with a conjunction. It is <u>not</u> a complete sentence and does not make sense on its own.

Try it

1 Underline the **subordinate clause** in the sentence.

The house was empty <u>when the family moved in</u>.

It began to rain <u>while we were on the mountain</u>.

The skeletons rattled <u>when they danced</u>.

Rover lay on the floor <u>as the ground shook</u>.

I was tired <u>before we reached the top of the hill</u>.

The room was cosy <u>although it was cold outside</u>.

2 Complete the **subordinate clause** after each **main clause**, using the conjunction in **bold**.

My sister laughed **when** she heard the joke.

The pirates watched **as** the ship headed towards them.

The moon rose **while** he was sleeping.

Bake the cake in the oven **until** it is golden brown.

She tried to grab the rope **before** it was too late.

Sentence practice

Write a sentence about a thief, using a **main clause** and a **subordinate clause**.

The thief dropped his bag of gold as he ran away.

33

Check that the pupils have underlined the conjunction as part of the subordinate clause.

These are just examples of subordinate clauses formed using the given conjunctions.

'Until' and 'before' can be used as conjunctions or prepositions. Check that the pupils have written a clause [including a verb] rather than just a word or phrase [e.g. until brown; before long]. If necessary, help them to reword answers [e.g. until it is brown]. [Note: This will be covered again in **Grammar 4** and **Grammar 5**.]

This is just an example of a suitable sentence, using a conjunction to add a subordinate clause to a main clause. Compare the pupils' answers, looking at the conjunctions used.

Lesson 23 Paragraphs: non-fiction

Focus using paragraphs to group together related ideas on a topic

Key terms **paragraph**, **heading**, **sub-heading**, sentence

Focus text Exercise helps you to stay fit and healthy. It is important that you do some exercise every day. You should eat a balanced diet. The more you use your body, the better it works.

TEACH

Show the focus text. Explain that this is a paragraph taken from an information text called 'Staying healthy'. Read it aloud. Ask the pupils which sentence does not belong in this paragraph and why [the one about a balanced diet – all the others are about exercise]. Cross out this sentence and ask the pupils to suggest another sentence that does fit the paragraph [e.g. Exercise works your muscles and makes your heart work better.].

Explain that paragraphs can be used to organise ideas in writing. A paragraph is a group of sentences that go together because they have one main idea or theme [e.g. in the focus text all the correctly placed sentences are about exercise].

Explain that when we write a non-fiction text about a subject, we divide the information up into different ideas and put each idea in a separate paragraph. There is no fixed number of sentences in a paragraph. It depends on how many related ideas we have – although paragraphs should not be too long.

A heading is used to show the subject of the text [what it is about]. Sometimes sub-headings are used to show the reader what each section or paragraph is about. Discuss a suitable sub-heading for the paragraph in the focus text [e.g. Exercise; Daily exercise]. Ask the pupils what other sub-headings might be used in the text 'Staying healthy' [e.g. Diet/Eating/Food; Avoiding germs].

EXTEND Discuss how information on 'Exercise' could be split into two paragraphs [e.g. one on the benefits; one on different types of exercise].

PRACTISE

Pupil book page 34

APPLY

- Use sub-headings to help the pupils develop their understanding of paragraphs. They could plan by grouping ideas under given or previously discussed sub-headings, and then refer to the plan when writing the report.
- The pupils write reports in science, geography or other subjects. After gathering together ideas using sub-headings, they then use paragraphs and sub-headings to present the information.
- The pupils plan and write letters to a pen friend, giving information about themselves. Ask the pupils to group ideas into three or four clear paragraphs [e.g. Me, My family, What I like, School].
- When they are evaluating their writing, encourage the pupils to identify any missing paragraph breaks or misplaced sentences.

ASSESS

Dictation: Swimming is a sport that is also great exercise. It is suitable for people of all ages.
Say: Complete this paragraph with two or three more sentences.
Answer: e.g. It exercises all parts of your body. Everyone should learn to swim as it can save your life.
Check: Look for paragraphs that continue the theme [the benefits of swimming], using correctly punctuated sentences.

Pupil book answers

Paragraphs: non-fiction

> **Remember**
>
> A **paragraph** is a group of **sentences** that go together because they have one main idea or theme.
>
> Exercise helps you to stay fit and healthy. It is important that you do some exercise every day. The more you use your body, the better it works.
>
> In non-fiction texts, **sub-headings** can show what a paragraph is about. The paragraph above could have the sub-heading 'Exercise'.

Try it

1 Here is the first sentence of a **paragraph**. Write <u>three</u> more sentences for this paragraph.

It is important to stay safe in the sun. Too much sun can be bad for you.

You should use sun cream to protect your skin from getting sunburnt.

You should also sit in the shade or wear a hat.

2 Here are some **sub-headings** for a report on materials. Write <u>two</u> sentences for each one.

Wood Wood comes from trees. Trees are cut down and made into things like tables and chairs.

Glass Glass is very useful because it is transparent. Lots of things are made from glass, such as windows and bottles.

Plastic Lots of things are made of plastic. Plastic is difficult to recycle, so it is bad for the environment.

Sentence practice

Write the first sentence for a **paragraph** about sheep in a report on farm animals.

34

Sheep are farm animals that give us wool and meat.

This is just an example of how the paragraph might develop using suitable ideas. Look for at least three additional sentences that give details about how or why. Look for the use of any conjunctions or prepositions to develop ideas. You could discuss this with the pupils.

Check that all sentences are demarcated correctly with capital letters and full stops.

This is just an example of how the paragraphs might develop using suitable ideas. Look for two relevant sentences under each sub-heading.

Again look to see if there is any use of conjunctions to develop ideas [e.g. because; so].

Check that all sentences are demarcated correctly with capital letters and full stops.

This is an example of an ideal opening sentence for a paragraph. It introduces the subject of the paragraph.

Lesson 24 **Paragraphs: stories and accounts**

> **Focus** using paragraphs starting with adverbs and prepositional phrases [to express time and place]
>
> **Key terms** paragraph, phrase, adverb, preposition, prepositional phrase
>
> **Focus text** Doctor Foster went to Gloucester.
> It began to rain.
> He fell in a puddle.
> The water was up to his middle.
>   ?
> He never went there again.

TEACH

Show the focus text. Explain that it shows the main events in a story. Read through the events. Ask: Do you recognise the story? [it is based on the nursery rhyme 'Doctor Foster'] Discuss the gap in the story. Ask: What is missing or not explained? [e.g. How did he get out of the puddle? Did someone help him? What did he do next? How did he get home?] Invite the pupils to suggest an extra event to fill the gap. Add at least one idea into the space to complete a story plan showing the main sequence of events.

Explain that when writing a story [or an account], we use paragraphs to help make clear the sequence of events. This helps the reader to follow the story. Explain that we start a new paragraph for each new event or when there is a shift in time or place. A plan of the events, like the focus text, helps us to see clearly when to start a new paragraph.

Explain that words and phrases can be used at the start of paragraphs to clearly signal the shifts in time and place. For example, we can use adverbs [e.g. soon; meanwhile; later; outside; nearby] or phrases starting with prepositions [e.g. at the same time; in a little while; after a long time; at the end of the road]. Explain that these special words and phrases need to be followed by a comma. [Note: Although using commas after fronted words and phrases is not covered until **Grammar 4**, it is a good idea to get the pupils into the habit.]

Invite the pupils to work through the events in the focus text, adding a word or phrase to show changes in time or place. [e.g. On Monday morning, …; In the afternoon, …; Outside the station, …; Immediately, …]

EXTEND Discuss how adverbs and prepositional phrases can also be used *within* a paragraph.

PRACTISE

Pupil book page 35

APPLY

- The pupils write the story of Doctor Foster, following the plan. They should use paragraphs starting with the adverbs and phrases. They then plan and write other stories based on events in nursery rhymes [e.g. Miss Muffet].
- The pupils plan stories based on other familiar stories. They should record the main events and then add suitable adverbs and phrases to lead into each paragraph of the story, showing where and when.
- The pupils plan accounts of events [e.g. personal experiences or historical events] in the same way.

ASSESS

Dictation: In the playground, Class 3 were waiting for the coach to arrive.
Say: Make a paragraph plan to show where they went, what happened and when.
Answer: Look for a list of ideas in a logical order with adverbs and/or phrases to show time and place.

Pupil book answers

Paragraphs: stories and accounts

Remember

In stories and accounts, you start a new **paragraph** for a new event or a change in time or place. **Adverbs** or **prepositional phrases** at the start of paragraphs can help to show these changes.

On Monday morning, Doctor Foster went to Gloucester.

Outside the station, he fell in a puddle.

Immediately, the water was up to his middle.

Try it

1 Here are the main events in a story. Underline the **adverbs** and **prepositional phrases** that show time or place.

One sunny day, Hare and Tortoise had a race.

Soon, Hare was way ahead.

At the top of the hill, Hare stopped for a sleep.

Eventually, Tortoise passed Hare.

After a long time, Hare woke up.

At the finishing line, Tortoise was waiting for Hare.

2 Imagine you are writing a story about a journey. Write **adverbs** and **phrases** for the start of **paragraphs** to show changes in time and place.

Time
On Saturday,
In the morning,
Suddenly,
Immediately,
After a while,

Place
At the station,
On the platform,
In our carriage,
On the journey,
Just past Broadstairs,

These are just examples of adverbs and prepositional phrases that might be used. Compare the pupils' choices.

Encourage the pupils to use commas after words and phrases like these when they are used at the start of paragraphs. Fronted words and phrases are covered in **Grammar 4**.

Sentence practice

Write the first **paragraph** of your story about a journey. Write on a new piece of paper.

35

Look for an opening paragraph that establishes who the story is about, using words and phrases to show time and place.

Lesson 25 **Root words**

Focus introducing root words with prefixes and suffixes

Key terms **root word**, prefix, suffix

Focus text Latest reaction to bank robbery
Unexpected discovery – prehistoric remains unearthed
Misleading statement about recycling

TEACH

Show the headlines in the focus text and discuss what each news story might be about.

Ask the pupils if they can see any words with prefixes [e.g. unexpected; misleading]. Spot the prefixes and circle them in colour [re–, un–, dis–, pre–, mis–]. Do the same with the suffixes, circling them in a different colour [–est, –ion, –ery, –ed, –ic, –ing, –ment].

Remind the pupils that many words are formed by adding a prefix or a suffix to a different word. Sometimes a prefix *and* a suffix are added to the same word to make a new word [e.g. re–act–ion].

Introduce the term 'root word'. Explain that the original word to which we add the prefixes and suffixes is called the root word [e.g. 'act' in 'reaction']. A root word cannot be broken down into any smaller words, so to find a root word we need to remove all the prefixes and suffixes.

Look at the words in the focus text and identify the root words. Use this activity to remind the pupils that sometimes the spelling of the root word changes when a suffix is added. For example, we sometimes remove the letter 'e' [e.g. recycle/recycling]; change the letter 'y' to 'i' [e.g. history/historic] or double the consonant [e.g. rob/robbery]. The pupils should be familiar with these rules from their spelling work. Remind the pupils that adding a suffix changes how a word is used, for example by making a verb into a noun [e.g. –ment makes the verb 'state' into the noun 'statement'].

Also discuss how the meaning of a root word is changed by adding a prefix [e.g. un– means 'the opposite'; mis– means 'wrongly'; re– means 'again' or 'back'].

EXTEND Discuss the root word in other less obvious examples [e.g. business].

PRACTISE

Pupil book page 36

APPLY

- When reading, encourage the pupils to use their knowledge of root words, prefixes and suffixes to help them work out the meaning of new words they meet.
- The pupils use knowledge of root words, prefixes and suffixes to help with spelling [e.g. cycle – bicycle].
- The pupils use dictionaries to find other words with prefixes [e.g. dis–; re–; mis–].
- In other subjects, challenge the pupils to identify the root word in subject-specific words [e.g. in history – tribal, invasion, kingdom, historic; in maths – addition, partition].
- Discuss how to use root words when looking up words in a dictionary.
- The pupils write headlines using root words with prefixes and suffixes [e.g. Replacement robotic arm!].

ASSESS

Dictation: There was a dis<u>agree</u>ment over the dis<u>allow</u>ed goal. The <u>manage</u>r will want no more mis<u>take</u>s in the re<u>play</u>.

Say: Look for words with prefixes and/or suffixes and underline the root word within each word.

Pupil book answers

Root words

Remember

Many words are formed by adding a **prefix** and/or a **suffix** to a **root word**. The root word is the original word without any prefixes or suffixes.

disagreement = dis agree ment

prefix   root word   suffix

Try it

1 Find the **root word** hidden in each of these longer words.

refreshments	fresh
ownership	own
enjoyable	joy
unavoidable	avoid
reawaken	wake
international	nation

Remind the pupils that the root word is the base word with all prefixes and suffixes removed [e.g. 'joy' rather than 'enjoy'].

2 Write <u>two</u> words that you can make by adding a **prefix** and/or a **suffix** to each root word.

build	builder	rebuilding
happy	unhappily	unhappiness
tidy	untidily	untidiness
friend	unfriendly	friendless
place	replacement	displace
lead	leader	misleading

There are other possibilities.

The words should be spelt correctly, including those that require a change in the spelling of the root word [e.g. happy; tidy].

Sentence practice

Add a **prefix** and a **suffix** to the root word 'cover'. Use the new word in a sentence.

We made an amazing discovery under the shed.

36

There are other words that can be formed from the root word 'cover' [e.g. uncovered; recovery]. The word should be spelt correctly and used in a suitable context.

Lesson 26 Word families

Focus introducing word families based on common words; seeing how the words are related in form and meaning

Key terms **word family**, root word

Focus text Meet my word family. Some of the words may be familiar.
Some may be unfamiliar.
Here is the horror family. They are horrible. One is horrid.
Another is horrific. They all behave horribly. They will horrify you.

TEACH

Show and read the first part of the focus text. Ask the pupils what they notice about the highlighted words [e.g. they share the root word 'family']. Discuss the meanings of the words 'familiar' and 'unfamiliar'.

Show the second part of the focus text and read it aloud. Ask the pupils what they notice about the highlighted words [e.g. they all look similar and have meanings that are linked to fear/terror/dread].

Introduce the term 'word family'. Explain that words belong to the same word family if they are based on the same root word [e.g. family, familiar, unfamiliar]. Sometimes the shared 'root' is not a recognisable word but part of a word [e.g. horrible, horror, horrid]. Words in the same word family are related, both in how they are formed [from the same root], and in their meaning.

Explain that the root word does not always look exactly the same in all the words in a word family – for example, the spelling might change if suffixes are added. However, the family relationship is clear in the word meanings – as in the 'horror' family, where all the words are to do with things that are horrible. Ask the pupils if they can suggest any other words in this word family. Or can they find other words in a dictionary? [e.g. horrendous; horridness; horridly; horrifying]

[Note: The idea of word 'roots' is explored in more detail in **Grammar 4**.]

EXTEND Explore the origin of word families [e.g. the 'horrible' family comes from a Latin word meaning 'hair standing on end']. Ask the pupils if they can see a link to the meaning today.

PRACTISE

Pupil book page 37

APPLY

- The pupils use dictionaries to help create word family trees, showing words related by form and meaning.
- In other subjects, explore word families related to current areas of study [e.g. in science – attract, attraction, attractive; dissolve, solve, solution; in maths – fractions, fracture].
- Encourage the pupils to use their knowledge of word families to help with spelling [e.g. oppose, opposite, opponent] and with working out the meaning of new words encountered when reading.

ASSESS

Dictation: It is hard to decide what to do but we must come to a decision soon.
Say: Underline the two words from the same word family. How do you know?
Answer: e.g. They are formed from the same root word and have related meanings.

Pupil book answers

Word families

Remember

A **word family** is a group of words that have related meanings. This is because they are all formed from the same **root word** – though the spelling of the root word might change slightly.

horrible   horrid   horrific

Try it

1   Draw a line to match each word to another word in the same **word family**.

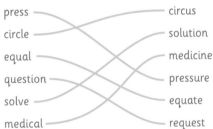

press ──── circus
circle ──── solution
equal ──── medicine
question ──── pressure
solve ──── equate
medical ──── request

2   Look at the <u>three</u> words in the **word family**. Write the **root word** of each family.

design   signature   signal   _sign_

cyclist   bicycle   cyclone   _cycle_

actor   action   react   _act_

fruity   fruitful   grapefruit   _fruit_

natural   supernatural   unnatural   _nature_

opposite   opponent   opposition   _oppose_

sensation   sensible   sensitive   _sense_

You could discuss with the pupils which root words stay the same and which change their spelling when a suffix is added [e.g. cycle; sense].

Sentence practice

Write a sentence using another word from the same **word family** as 'terror'.

There was a terrible storm last night.   37

The pupils could use a dictionary to find words related to terror [e.g. terrible; terrify; terrifying]. Remind them to think about the meaning of words as well as their formation. Not every word beginning 'terr' is related to the word 'terror' [e.g. terrace, terrapin]. Interestingly, though, 'terrific' is! The original meaning was 'causing terror'.

Lesson 27 Word classes

Focus exploring words with different meanings and functions in different contexts

Key terms noun, verb, adjective, adverb, **word class**

Focus text The horse is fit and well.
The bucket will not fit in the well.
The team must train well for the match.

TEACH

Show the first sentence of the focus text and read it aloud. Discuss what image it brings to mind [e.g. a healthy horse]. Ask what type of word is highlighted and what the words mean [adjectives – they tell us more about the horse; they mean healthy].

Show the next sentence. Ask: What image does it bring to mind? What do the words 'fit' and 'well' mean here? What types of words are they? ['fit' is a verb – an action; 'well' is a noun – it names something]

Show the third sentence, again discussing the image created and the meaning of the highlighted words. Ask: What types of words are they? ['train' is a verb; 'well' is an adverb – it tells us more about the verb]

Remind the pupils that some words have more than one meaning but look and sound the same. These words are called homonyms. [Note: Homonyms are covered in **Grammar 6**. The pupils do not need to know this term yet but you can introduce it here if you wish.] These words can function in different ways in different sentences. This means they can belong to different word classes or types of word [e.g. 'well' is an adjective in the first sentence, a noun in the second and an adverb in the third].

Discuss how the pupils worked out the image and meaning required for each sentence. Establish that it is the context of the sentence – the other words around the uncertain word – that helps us work out which meaning to choose. The sentence context also tells us whether the word is a verb, noun, adjective or adverb. So, for example, in the third sentence we know that 'train' is a verb because of where it comes in the sentence; this meaning also fits with other words in the sentence [team, match]. Explain to the pupils that they should always look at how a word is used in the sentence when deciding on what type of word it is.

Invite the pupils to suggest a sentence showing the word 'train' used as a noun or the word 'match' used as a verb [e.g. I caught the train at the station. Your red top matches my boots.].

EXTEND Explore words with different meanings and different pronunciations [e.g. bow].

PRACTISE

Pupil book page 38

APPLY

* When reading, look for words with alternative meanings and discuss with the pupils how the context of the sentence helps to work out the correct meaning and word class.
* In other subject areas, discuss subject-specific meanings of words [e.g. in science, a table might be used to record results].
* The pupils read and/or write some humorous verse or wordplay using homonyms [e.g. Did you see the sea wave?].

ASSESS

Dictation: I <u>saw</u> the boy <u>bat</u> the ball away.
Say: Underline the two verbs in the sentence. Then write two more sentences using these words as nouns.
Answer: e.g. I need a saw to cut the wood. A bat flew across the night sky.

Pupil book answers

Word classes

> **Remember**
>
> Words can be **nouns**, **verbs**, **adjectives** or **adverbs**. Some words have more than one meaning and belong to more than one **word class**. You need to look at the rest of the sentence to work out what the word means and what type of word it is.
>
>
>
> The horse is fit and well.   (adjectives)
> The bucket will not fit in the well. (verb and noun)
> The team trained well.   (adverb)

Try it

1 Read the sentence. What type of word is underlined? Write '**noun**', '**verb**' or '**adjective**'.

<u>Ring</u> the door bell of flat one.	verb
She wore a gold <u>ring</u> and a silver watch.	noun
<u>Watch</u> my bag for me and keep it safe.	verb
The man kept the form in the <u>safe</u>.	noun
People began to <u>form</u> a queue.	verb
I had the <u>last</u> slice of cake.	adjective

2 Underline the **word** in each sentence that has another meaning. Write a sentence to show the other meaning.

The flames <u>rose</u> into the sky. I picked a red rose from the bush.

Joe had a <u>spot</u> on his nose. I like to spot birds in the garden.

A feather is really <u>light</u>. I switched on the light.

These are examples of sentences showing a different meaning of the word. Accept other answers showing different meanings [e.g. The dress was rose-coloured.].

Sentences should be correctly punctuated.

Sentence practice

Write a sentence using the word 'wave' as a **verb**. Write another sentence using the word 'wave' as a **noun**.

verb They wave a flag at the end of a race.

noun A big wave crashed on to the rocks.

38

These are examples of sentences showing different functions of the word 'wave'. The first sentence should use it as a verb. The second sentence should use it as a noun [including 'a wave of the hand'].

Sentences should be correctly punctuated.

Lesson 28 **Pronouns**

Focus introducing pronouns and their function; using personal pronouns to avoid repetition

Key terms noun, proper noun, **pronoun**

Focus text Grace saw Edward but Grace did not speak to Edward. Edward completely ignored Grace until Grace went away.

Grace saw Edward but she did not speak to him. He completely ignored her until she went away.

TEACH

Show the first part of the focus text. Read it aloud and discuss why it sounds awkward [e.g. it keeps repeating the characters' names]. Reveal and read the second version. Ask: Why does this sound better? [e.g. less repetition; words like 'she', 'her', 'he', 'him' are used in place of the names; it is shorter]

Introduce the term 'pronoun'. Explain that pronouns are words that are used in place of nouns or proper nouns [names]. They are useful because they stop us from having to repeat the same name or noun too many times, as shown in the focus text.

Look at the pronouns in the focus text and discuss which words they replace. 'She'/'her' [female pronouns] replace 'Grace', and 'he'/'him' [male pronouns] replace 'Edward'. Discuss what would happen if Grace had a friend with her [e.g. Grace and Ellie saw Edward ...]. Ask: What pronouns would be used then? [plural pronouns – 'they'/'them']. What if it were, 'I saw Edward ...' or 'Grace and I saw Edward ...'? [first person pronouns – 'I'/'me'; 'we'/'us']

Explain that we use the pronoun 'it' if it is a thing rather than a person [e.g. They had an <u>argument</u> yesterday. They don't want to talk about <u>it</u>.].

[Note: This lesson focuses on personal pronouns. Other types of pronoun are introduced in **Grammar 4** and **5**.]

EXTEND Discuss the position of the pronouns within a sentence [e.g. I/he/she/we/they – before the verb; me/him/her/us/them – after the verb].

PRACTISE

Pupil book page 39

APPLY

- When reading together, discuss who the pronouns refer to.
- Before they begin writing a personal account, discuss with the pupils what pronouns could be used [I/me; we/us]. Do the same when writing a third-person account or story [he/she; they/them].
- The pupils revise writing, together with a writing partner, to check when it might be better to use a pronoun rather than repeating a name.
- The pupils write an incident from a story, changing the main character from a male to a female character [or female to male]. Discuss the change in pronouns needed.
- Discuss when the pronoun 'you' is needed in writing [e.g. in instructions – You will need ...; in letters – I am writing to you ...].

ASSESS

Dictation: Jess was annoyed with the twins but the twins just smiled at Jess.
Say: Rewrite the sentence using pronouns in place of the nouns and proper nouns.
Answer: She was annoyed with them but they just smiled at her.

Pupil book answers

Pronouns

Remember

Pronouns are words that take the place of **nouns** or proper nouns.
They help you to avoid repeating the same noun.

<u>Grace</u> saw <u>Edward</u> but <u>Grace</u> did not speak to <u>Edward</u>.

<u>Grace</u> saw <u>Edward</u> but she did not speak to him.

Try it

1. Underline all the **pronouns** in each sentence.

   The woman saw that <u>we</u> were hungry so <u>she</u> gave <u>us</u> some bread.

   The people ran away from the tiger when <u>they</u>
   saw <u>it</u> coming.

   Jack and <u>I</u> said <u>we</u> would help <u>them</u>.

   Was Fatima at home when <u>you</u> went to see <u>her</u>?

   Max found the book and <u>he</u> gave <u>it</u> to <u>me</u>.

   <u>I</u> saw Harry and <u>I</u> spoke to <u>him</u>.

2. Rewrite the sentences using **pronouns** in place of the underlined nouns or
   noun phrases.

   <u>Kofi and I</u> waved to <u>Doug</u> but <u>Doug</u> did not see <u>Kofi and me</u>.

   We waved to him but he did not see us.

   <u>Dad</u> told <u>Mum</u> about the cat but <u>Mum</u> did not believe <u>Dad</u>.

   He told her about the cat but she did not believe him.

   <u>Tia and Shona</u> found a shell and took <u>the shell</u> home with <u>Tia and Shona</u>.

   They found a shell and took it home with them.

Sentence practice

Write a sentence using the **pronouns** 'he' and 'it'. Make sure it is clear
who or what the pronouns refer to.

Mark had a pencil but he dropped it on the floor.

This is just an example of a sentence using the given
pronouns to replace nouns. Make sure it is clear from
the sentences who or what the pronouns refer to.

Lesson 29 Pronouns and verbs

Focus grammatical agreement of pronouns and verbs; revising contracted forms of verbs

Key terms pronoun, proper noun, noun, verb, contraction

Focus text Buster is sitting with his family. They are all watching television. Buster likes this programme. He has seen it before. Buster barks in approval.

TEACH

Show the focus text and read it aloud. Discuss who it is about [Buster – a dog]. Ask: What types of word are highlighted? [nouns – Buster, his family; the associated pronouns – he, they].

Introduce the idea of rewriting the text as if Buster is writing it himself [i.e. in the first person]. [Note: The pupils are not required to know the terms 'first person' and 'third person', but you can introduce them if you wish.] Rewrite each sentence, discussing how the highlighted words need to be changed [Buster – I; his – my; they – we; he – I]. See if the pupils notice that the verbs also need to change [I am, I like, I have, I bark]. If not, read the sentence aloud and discuss why it does not sound right [e.g. I is sitting …; I likes …].

Explain that a verb must match, or agree with, the noun or pronoun that comes before it. Discuss examples of these differences in the focus text [e.g. 'is' with 'he'/'she' (singular pronouns); 'are' with 'we'/'they' (plural pronouns); 'am' with 'I' only]. Remind the pupils to say or read sentences aloud to check that the correct verb is used after a pronoun.

Once the first-person version is complete, read it aloud. Introduce the idea of using some contractions to make it sound more informal. Discuss which words could be contracted [I am, We are, I have]. Explain that these contractions involve pronouns and verbs. When we write the contractions, the verb is contracted but the pronoun remains intact [I'm, We're, I've]. Ask the pupils to explain where the apostrophe goes [in place of the missing letters in the verb].

Invite the pupils to orally compose another sentence for the focus text using a pronoun–verb contraction [e.g. It's a good programme.].

EXTEND Discuss non-Standard English spoken forms sometimes used in speech [e.g. We <u>was</u> watching television].

PRACTISE

Pupil book page 40

APPLY

- The pupils change a short third-person account of an event into a first-person account using 'I' and 'we' rather than 'he'/'she'/'they'. Remind them to make the necessary changes to verbs.
- The pupils write an incident from a story as a first-person account. They then check their use of pronouns and verbs.
- The pupils write diaries based on real or imaginary events, using contractions to sound informal.
- The pupils work with a partner to proofread their own writing, checking verb and pronoun agreement.
- In other subjects [e.g. history], find opportunities for the pupils to write in the first person as well as the third person [e.g. letters from or about historical characters or events].

ASSESS

Dictation: She likes reading. She is always reading something. She has loads of books.

Say: Rewrite these sentences using the pronoun 'I'.

Answer: I like reading. I am always reading something. I have loads of books.

Pupil book answers

Pronouns and verbs

Remember

When you use a **pronoun**, you must also use the correct form of the **verb** to follow it.

He <u>is</u> sitting.   He <u>likes</u> this.   He <u>has</u> seen it.

I <u>am</u> sitting.   I <u>like</u> this.   I <u>have</u> seen it.

Try it

1   Write the correct form of the **verb** for each **pronoun**.

I <u>was</u> late. They <u>were</u> early.   (was were)

She <u>chooses</u> a red flag. I <u>choose</u> a blue one.   (choose chooses)

He <u>does</u> his homework. I <u>do</u> mine.   (do does)

We <u>are</u> lost. I <u>am</u> scared.   (am are is)

They <u>have</u> lots of money. He <u>has</u> none.   (has have)

I <u>like</u> jam and she <u>likes</u> honey.   (like likes)

2   Rewrite each sentence using the **pronoun** 'I' instead of 'he' or 'she'. Check that you have used the correct form of each **verb**.

He has walked for miles and he is starving.

<u>I have walked for miles and I am starving.</u>

He does the washing up and he tidies the kitchen.

<u>I do the washing up and I tidy the kitchen.</u>

She's out at the moment but she'll be back soon.

<u>I'm out at the moment but I'll be back soon.</u>

In the third sentence, check for correct spelling and correct placement of the apostrophes.

Check that all sentences are correctly punctuated, including capital letters for the pronoun 'I'.

Sentence practice

Write <u>two</u> sentences to describe yourself. Use the correct **verbs** with the pronoun 'I'.

<u>I have short black hair and brown eyes. I am tall for my age.</u>

40

This is just an example.

Check that both sentences are correctly punctuated.

Lesson 30 Singular and plural nouns

Focus singular and plural nouns; introducing irregular plural nouns

Key terms singular, plural, noun, verb

Focus text The king asks his son. His son asks the servant. The servant asks the wise man. The wise man asks the lady. The lady asks the child. The child asks the sheep. The sheep asks a fox. The fox asks an owl. The owl asks a mouse.

TEACH

Show the focus text. Discuss who and how many characters are asked the king's question.

Look at the highlighted nouns. Ask the pupils if these are singular or plural nouns [singular – there is no –s/–es added]. Invite the pupils to help you change all the nouns after 'king' into plurals, so that more people are asked. Work through the text, discussing the changes needed. Sometimes the only change will be to add –s/–es [sons, servants, foxes, owls]. Sometimes other changes are needed [man/men, lady/ladies, child/children, mouse/mice].

Remind the pupils that nouns can be singular [just one] or plural [more than one]. Most nouns are made into plurals by adding –s/–es; sometimes this involves a change in spelling [e.g. lady/ladies]. However, there are some plurals that do not end –s/–es [e.g. men; children; mice]. There are also a few nouns that are the same in the plural as in the singular [e.g. sheep].

As you change the nouns to plurals, read each sentence and discuss other words that need to be changed [e.g. verb endings – his son asks/his sons ask]. Remind the pupils that plural nouns need the plural form of the verb.

Point out that you will also need to change 'a'/'an' to 'the' or another determiner [e.g. a fox/the foxes; an owl/some owls]. Explain that 'a'/'an' is used with singular nouns but not with plurals [e.g. not 'a foxes']. It has to be changed to 'the', which can be used with singular or plural nouns.

EXTEND Discuss other unusual plurals, including words that are always plurals [e.g. trousers; scissors].

PRACTISE

Pupil book page 41

APPLY

- The pupils write accounts or stories set in a crowded place. They should plan by noting useful plural nouns and noun phrases [e.g. people; noisy children; women; men with baskets; ladies with trolleys].
- In maths, the pupils write problems to solve, using plural forms of nouns [e.g. share fifteen sweets between three children; share a hundred sheep between two fields].
- Draw attention to interesting plurals in other subjects [e.g. in science – woodlice, leaves, teeth].
- Use writing frames to encourage the use of singular and plural forms when writing information texts [e.g. Teeth are ...; A tooth is ...].
- When revising a piece of writing, encourage the pupils to check the use of verbs with singular and plural nouns.

ASSESS

Dictation: The child enjoyed doing the puzzle and the quiz.
Say: Rewrite the sentence using plural nouns.
Answer: The children enjoyed doing the puzzles and the quizzes.

Pupil book answers

Singular and plural nouns

Remember

Most **nouns** are made into **plurals** by adding **–s** or **–es**. Sometimes the spelling of the noun changes when you add the plural ending.

lady – ladies

Some plural nouns do not end **–s** or **–es**.

man – men   woman – women   child – children

Try it

1 Write the **plural** of these **singular nouns**.

horse	horses	pony	ponies
beetle	beetles	woodlouse	woodlice
puppy	puppies	kitten	kittens
goose	geese	turkey	turkeys
sheep	sheep	fox	foxes

Check that the plural nouns are spelt correctly.

2 Rewrite each sentence, making all the **nouns** into **plurals**.

The mouse was eating the berry off the bush.

The mice were eating the berries off the bushes.

The witch had a bad foot and a rotten tooth.

The witches had bad feet and rotten teeth.

Did the deer under the tree have a white patch?

Did the deer under the trees have white patches?

Check that the plural nouns are spelt correctly.

In the first sentence, check that 'was' is changed to 'were'. In the second and third sentences, check that 'a' is not used with the plural noun. The pupils may have used a word such as 'some' instead [e.g. some white patches].

Sentence practice

Write a sentence using the **plural** of the **nouns** 'child', 'jelly', 'party'.

The children had red and green jellies at their birthday parties.

This is just an example of a sentence using the plural nouns. The plural nouns should be spelt correctly.

41

Revision 3 answers

> This page revises punctuation covered in this book. The pupils should be encouraged to proofread their own writing to check this punctuation. The focus of each activity is given to help identify areas that may need further reinforcement.

Focus: apostrophes in contracted forms

Both spelling and the placement of the apostrophes need to be correct.

Check that answers start with capital letters as they are at the start of the sentence.

Focus: commas in lists

Check that there is no comma before 'and'.

Focus: inverted commas and end punctuation in direct speech

Check that the end punctuation of the spoken words is inside the inverted commas.

Grammar 3

Revision 3

1 Write the underlined words in each sentence as a **contraction** by using an **apostrophe**.

You will never believe what happened.   You'll

We are coming to see you on Sunday.   We're

Here is a list of questions.   Here's

I have been learning a new song.   I've

2 Rewrite this sentence with the correct **punctuation**.

You will need two ripe peaches a sliced apple some orange segments and a few green grapes.

You will need two ripe peaches, a sliced apple, some orange segments and a few green grapes.

3 Add the missing **punctuation marks** in each sentence of **direct speech**.

"I am so lonely," said the little elf.

"Help!" yelled the girl.

"I can help you find the key," the wizard said.

"What is your favourite film?" asked Shazana.

4 Rewrite each sentence with the correct **punctuation**.

My teachers name is mr andrews.   My teacher's name is Mr Andrews.

Annies dog is called rex.   Annie's dog is called Rex.

Is the tigers name maya?   Is the tiger's name Maya?

Dads new car will come on friday.   Dad's new car will come on Friday.

42

Focus: apostrophes for possession; capital letters for proper nouns

Although the main focus is on adding the apostrophe for possession, the pupils also need to add capital letters at the start of proper nouns.

This reflects the proofreading that the pupils should do with their own writing, where they will often be checking for more than one type of punctuation.

This page revises terms and concepts introduced in this book. The focus of each activity is given to help you identify areas that might need further reinforcement.

Grammar 3

⑤ Add the verbs needed to complete each sentence below.

I ___have___ been to school.

Mum ___has___ been to work.

Now we ___are___ having tea.

Dad ___is___ having spaghetti and I ___am___ having pizza.

He ___is___ going home and I ___am___ going shopping.

⑥ Complete each sentence to say <u>where</u>. Use at least <u>one</u> preposition in each sentence.

The pirates buried the treasure ___under the palm tree.___

Ahmed saw the game he wanted ___in the shop window.___

He hid the sack ___behind the shed at the bottom of the garden.___

She put the plant ___on the table in the sunlight.___

⑦ Add an adverb to say <u>when</u> this event happened.

Uncle Colin arrived ___yesterday___ .

Add an adverb to say <u>where</u> the event happened.

Uncle Colin arrived ___here___ .

⑧ Add a subordinate clause to complete each sentence. Use a different conjunction each time.

I packed my bag ___before I went to school.___

The car came to a sudden stop ___when it crashed into a lamppost.___

He took his umbrella ___because it looked like rain.___

They sat on the river bank ___until the sky went dark.___

Focus: conjunctions to express time and cause

These are just examples of conjunctions and clauses that could be used. Compare the pupils' answers and discuss how different conjunctions affect the meaning of the sentence.

Check that a subordinate clause is added using a subordinating conjunction, rather than a phrase or another main clause using the conjunctions 'and' or 'but'. [Note: The pupils will learn more about this in **Grammar 4**.]

Focus: present perfect and progressive forms of verbs

Remind the pupils to read the sentences aloud to see if they sound right.

Focus: prepositions to express place

These are just examples of suitable phrases beginning with prepositions. The third and fourth sentences show how two prepositions might be used.

Compare the pupils' answers and discuss how their choices affect the meaning of the sentence.

Focus: adverbs to express time and place

These are just examples of suitable adverbs. There are other possibilities [e.g. arrived earlier; arrived home; arrived there; arrived outside].

Make sure the pupils have used an adverb rather than a prepositional phrase [e.g. on Monday; at the house].

43

Writing task 3: Analysis sheet

Tick the circles to show amount of evidence found in writing:
1 No evidence
2 Some evidence
3 Clear evidence

Pupil name: _____

Date: _____

Assessing punctuation

The writing sample demonstrates:	Evidence		
sentence boundaries demarcated with capital letters and full stops.	(1)	(2)	(3)
question marks and exclamation marks used appropriately when required.	(1)	(2)	(3)
capital letters used for 'I' and proper nouns [names of characters, places, the boat].	(1)	(2)	(3)
commas used to separate items in a list [e.g. They were cold, wet and hungry.].	(1)	(2)	(3)
apostrophes used in contracted forms [e.g. we're sinking] or for singular possession [e.g. Dad's boat].	(1)	(2)	(3)
inverted commas used to indicate direct speech [e.g. "What can you see?" he asked.].	(1)	(2)	(3)

Assessing grammar and sentence structure

The writing sample demonstrates:	Evidence		
grammatically correct sentences [including nouns, pronouns and verb agreement].	(1)	(2)	(3)
different sentence types [statements, commands, exclamations, questions].	(1)	(2)	(3)
co-ordinating conjunctions [and, but, or] to link sentences.	(1)	(2)	(3)
subordinating conjunctions to show time or cause [e.g. The children were scared when …].	(1)	(2)	(3)
correct and consistent use of past tense, including progressive and perfect forms.	(1)	(2)	(3)
adverbs and prepositions to link events and add detail [e.g. in the bottom of the boat; after an hour; suddenly].	(1)	(2)	(3)
adjectives and expanded noun phrases to add detail and describe settings and characters [e.g. murky water; frightened voice].	(1)	(2)	(3)

Key target: _____

Writing task 3: Pupil checklist

Name: _____   Date: _____

Reread what you have written to check that it makes sense. Tick the circle if you have correctly used the punctuation or grammar feature in your writing.

Punctuation

◯ I have used capital letters at the beginning of sentences.

◯ I have used full stops at the end of sentences.

◯ I have used question marks or exclamation marks where they are needed.

◯ I have used capital letters for 'I' and any names.

◯ I have used commas to separate items in a list.

◯ I have used apostrophes in contracted forms (e.g. we're sinking) and for possession (e.g. Dad's boat).

◯ I have used inverted commas for direct speech (e.g. "What can you see?" he asked.).

Grammar and sentences

◯ I have written in sentences and checked that they sound right (e.g. checking verbs and pronouns).

◯ I have used different types of sentence (e.g. statements, questions, exclamations, commands).

◯ I have used the conjunctions 'and', 'but', 'or' to make some longer sentences.

◯ I have used conjunctions to say when or why (e.g. when, before, after, while, as, because, since).

◯ I have used the past tense to write about what happened.

◯ I have used adverbs and prepositions to say where, when or how (e.g. suddenly, in the bottom of the boat).

◯ I have used adjectives and longer noun phrases to describe characters, settings and events.

Teacher feedback

```



```

My key target: _____

_____

Final test

Name: _____

1 Tick the sentence below that is <u>not</u> a **command**.

Write a letter to your friend. ☐

Then put it in an envelope. ☐

You will need to write the address. ☐

Stick a stamp on the envelope. ☐

1 mark

2 Underline the **noun phrase** in this sentence.

He was very excited to meet the famous singer.

1 mark

3 Write the form of the **adjective** 'interesting' needed to compare the two books.

This book is _____ than that one.

1 mark

4 Underline all the words in this sentence that should start with a **capital letter**.

on tuesday, mr elliot took his class to chester to learn about the romans.

1 mark

5 Write 'a' or 'an' to complete each **noun phrase**.

_____ wise owl

_____ empty box

_____ orange umbrella

_____ slippery eel

1 mark

From: **Grammar 3 Teacher's Guide** © *Schofield & Sims Ltd, 2017. This page may be photocopied after purchase.*

6 Look at where the arrow is pointing. Which **punctuation mark** is missing?

"Follow me," shouted Alvin Then he turned and ran off down the road.

↑

comma ☐   exclamation mark ☐

full stop ☐   question mark ☐

☐
1 mark

7 Add <u>two</u> **past tense verbs** to complete this sentence.

Alex _____ walking down the lane when he _____ a voice.

☐
1 mark

8 Rewrite this sentence using an **apostrophe** correctly.

My friend Toms eyes are green. _____

☐
1 mark

9 Complete the sentence by adding <u>three</u> more items that you will buy. Remember to **punctuate** your sentence correctly.

I am going to the shop to buy an exercise book _____

_____

☐
1 mark

10 Tick the correct box to show whether the underlined word is a **verb**, **noun** or **adjective**.

	Verb	Noun	Adjective
The ship hit a <u>rock</u>.			
The ship began to <u>rock</u>.			
The road was <u>rocky</u>.			

☐
1 mark

11 Write the **contracted form** of the underlined words, using an **apostrophe**.

I know <u>we are</u> going to have a good time. <u>You will</u> see.

_____   _____

1 mark

12 Complete this sentence with a **conjunction**.

He had a lie-in _____ it was Saturday.

1 mark

13 What type of word is underlined in the sentence below?

We went to the library <u>after</u> school.

conjunction ☐

adverb ☐

preposition ☐

adjective ☐

1 mark

14 Add the correct **verb** to complete the sentences below.

Harry _____ gone out to play.

They _____ waited an hour so far.

1 mark

15 Draw a line to match each **prefix** to the correct word.

mis	clockwise
anti-	store
super	understanding
sub	time
over	title

1 mark

16 Underline the <u>three</u> **adverbs** in the sentence below.

It is raining heavily outside but I think it will stop soon.

1 mark

17 Insert the **inverted commas** in the correct places in the sentence below.

It was not my fault, said Sophie.

1 mark

18 Tick <u>one</u> box to show the **main clause** in this sentence.

<u>All of a sudden,</u> <u>the genie appeared</u> <u>in a puff</u> <u>of green smoke</u>.

1 mark

19 Complete this sentence with a word from the same **word family** as the underlined word.

We are trying to <u>solve</u> the problem. We hope to find a _____ soon.

1 mark

20 Add a **subordinate clause** to the sentence below.

I took the dog for a walk _____

1 mark

End of test

Final test: Mark scheme

Q	Focus	Answer
1	identifying sentence types: commands	**Award 1 mark** for the correct box ticked. You will need to write the address. ✓
2	noun phrases	**Award 1 mark** for the full noun phrase underlined. He was very excited to meet <u>the famous singer</u>.
3	using adjectives to compare	**Award 1 mark** for the correct form of the adjective. This book is more interesting than that one.
4	capital letters for names and start of sentence	**Award 1 mark** for all <u>six</u> words correctly underlined. <u>on</u> <u>tuesday</u>, <u>mr</u> <u>elliot</u> took his class to <u>chester</u> to learn about the <u>romans</u>.
5	using 'a' or 'an'	**Award 1 mark** for all <u>four</u> correct. <u>a</u> wise owl <u>an</u> empty box <u>an</u> orange umbrella <u>a</u> slippery eel
6	demarcating sentences with full stops	**Award 1 mark** for the correct box ticked. full stop ✓
7	simple past tense; progressive past tense	**Award 1 mark** for <u>both</u> words supplied and spelt correctly. Alex <u>was</u> walking down the lane when he <u>heard</u> a voice.
8	apostrophe for singular possession	**Award 1 mark** for a sentence with an apostrophe added correctly. My friend Tom's eyes are green. The sentence must have a capital letter and full stop.
9	commas in lists	**Award 1 mark** for a sentence that lists <u>four</u> items and uses correct punctuation, e.g. I am going to the shop to buy an exercise book, a pencil case, a new pen and some crayons.
10	identifying word classes: nouns, verbs, adjectives	**Award 1 mark** for all <u>three</u> correct. <table><tr><td></td><td>Verb</td><td>Noun</td><td>Adjective</td></tr><tr><td>The ship hit a <u>rock</u>.</td><td></td><td>✓</td><td></td></tr><tr><td>The ship began to <u>rock</u>.</td><td>✓</td><td></td><td></td></tr><tr><td>The road was <u>rocky</u>.</td><td></td><td></td><td>✓</td></tr></table>
11	apostrophe to mark contracted forms	**Award 1 mark** for <u>both</u> words written correctly. we're You'll Correct spelling and correct placement of the apostrophe is required. 'You'll' must be written with a capital letter as it is at the start of a sentence.
12	conjunctions to express time and cause	**Award 1 mark** for a conjunction that makes a grammatically correct sentence, e.g. He had a lie-in <u>as</u> it was Saturday.

13	prepositions to express time	**Award 1 mark** for the correct box ticked. preposition ✓
14	present perfect form of verbs	**Award 1 mark** for <u>both</u> verbs supplied and spelt correctly. Harry <u>has</u> gone out to play. They <u>have</u> waited an hour so far.
15	forming words with prefixes [e.g. super–, anti–]	**Award 1 mark** for all <u>five</u> pairs correctly matched. mis ——— clockwise anti- —— store super —— understanding sub —— time over —— title
16	–ly adverbs; adverbs to express time and place	**Award 1 mark** for all <u>three</u> words correctly underlined. It is raining <u>heavily</u> <u>outside</u> but I think it will stop <u>soon</u>.
17	inverted commas to indicate direct speech	**Award 1 mark** for all inverted commas inserted correctly. "It was not my fault," said Sophie.
18	identifying clauses	**Award 1 mark** for the correct box ticked. <u>the genie appeared</u> ✓
19	word families based on common words	**Award 1 mark** for either word. solution/resolution
20	subordinating conjunctions and subordinate clauses	**Award 1 mark** for a grammatically correct sentence containing a subordinate clause and using correct punctuation, e.g. I took the dog for a walk <u>while Mum was having a rest</u>. I took the dog for a walk <u>because he needed exercise</u>. I took the dog for a walk <u>before it got too dark</u>. *Do not accept* sentences that use a phrase instead of a subordinate clause [e.g. I took the dog for a walk before tea.]; or responses that add another main clause [e.g. I took the dog for a walk and it began to rain.].

Final test: Analysis sheet

Tick the box for each correct answer.

Q	Focus	Pupil names									
1	identifying sentence types: commands										
2	noun phrases										
3	using adjectives to compare										
4	capital letters for names and start of sentence										
5	using 'a' or 'an'										
6	demarcating sentences with full stops										
7	simple past tense; progressive past tense										
8	apostrophe for singular possession										
9	commas in lists										
10	identifying word classes: nouns, verbs, adjectives										
11	apostrophe to mark contracted forms										
12	conjunctions to express time and cause										
13	prepositions to express time										
14	present perfect form of verbs										
15	forming words with prefixes [e.g. super–, anti–]										
16	–ly adverbs; adverbs to express time and place										
17	inverted commas to indicate direct speech										
18	identifying clauses										
19	word families based on common words										
20	subordinating conjunctions and subordinate clauses										
Total correct answers per pupil											

Target tracking sheet

Group: _____

Target: _____

Date set: _____ Date for review: _____

Tick the circles to show depth of understanding:
1 Just beginning
2 Progressing
3 Learning is embedded

Pupil name	Evidence from independent writing	Progress in independent writing
		① ② ③
		① ② ③
		① ② ③
		① ② ③
		① ② ③
		① ② ③
		① ② ③
		① ② ③
		① ② ③
		① ② ③

Learning pathways sheet

Pupil name: _____

Date last updated: _____

Tick the circles to show depth of understanding:
1 Just beginning
2 Progressing
3 Learning is embedded

Punctuation pathway

Recognise and demarcate sentence boundaries with capital letters and full stops.
① ② ③

Use question marks and exclamation marks to demarcate different sentence types.
① ② ③

Use capital letters for 'I' and all proper nouns [names of people and places, days of the week].
① ② ③

Use commas to separate items in a list.
① ② ③

Use apostrophes in shortened [contracted] forms.
① ② ③

Use apostrophes for [singular] possession.
① ② ③

Use inverted commas and other punctuation to indicate direct speech.
① ② ③

Grammar and sentence pathway

Use different sentence types correctly: command, question, exclamation, statement.
① ② ③

Use the conjunctions 'and', 'but', 'or' to join ideas and create longer sentences.
① ② ③

Use past and present tense, including progressive and perfect verb forms.
① ② ③

Use a range of subordinating conjunctions to add more detail to a sentence.
① ② ③

Use adjectives and expanded noun phrases to describe, specify and give more detail.
① ② ③

Use adverbs and prepositions to add detail about where, when and how.
① ② ③

Use pronouns to avoid repetition.
① ② ③

Glossary

Adjective
An **adjective** is a word used to modify or specify a noun [e.g. an <u>angry</u> man; the <u>red</u> car; a <u>beautiful</u> day].
Lesson 3
- **Comparative** and **superlative adjectives** are used to compare nouns. The suffixes –er and –est are added to shorter adjectives [e.g. the faster car; the fastest car]. The words 'more' and 'most' are used with longer adjectives [e.g. a more expensive car; the most expensive car]. Lesson 7
- Some adjectives are formed by adding a suffix to a word [e.g. care<u>ful</u>; care<u>less</u>].
- Some adjectives are formed by adding both a suffix and a prefix to a word [e.g. <u>un</u>remark<u>able</u>]. Grammar 4

Adverb
An **adverb** is a word that modifies a verb or action in a sentence. An adverb can specify *how, where,* or *when* the action took place [e.g. He arrived <u>quietly</u>. He arrived <u>outside</u>. He arrived <u>yesterday</u>.].
- Sometimes adverbs modify other words, such as another adverb [e.g. really quickly] or an adjective [e.g. a really good idea]. Lessons 11 and 12
- Some adverbs are used to show links between ideas or events [e.g. 'meanwhile' shows a time link; 'therefore' shows the result of an action]. Lesson 24

Adverbials will be covered in Grammar 4.

Apostrophe
An **apostrophe ['']** is a punctuation mark with two different uses:
- it shows the position of missing letters in **contractions** or shortened forms of words that are often used in informal speech [e.g. can't; who's; we've]. Lesson 6
- it is used with the letter 's' to show **possession** in the possessive form of nouns [e.g. Sam's hat]. Lesson 6
- If the noun is plural and already ends in –s, the apostrophe is added by itself, <u>after</u> the –s [e.g. the parents' meeting]. For irregular plurals not ending in –s, an apostrophe and an 's' are added [e.g. children's playground]. Grammar 4

Article
The words 'the', 'a' and 'an' are **articles**. Lesson 4
- 'The' is the **definite article**. It shows that the noun that it precedes is known [e.g. <u>the</u> dog].
- 'A' or 'an' are **indefinite articles**. They show that the noun that they precede is unknown [e.g. <u>a</u> cat, <u>an</u> elephant]. 'An' is used before a word beginning with a vowel sound.

Articles are a type of **determiner**. Determiners will be covered in Grammar 4.

Clause

A **clause** is a group of words that are connected together and include a verb. A clause can be a complete sentence or part of a sentence. Lesson 21

- A **main clause** is a clause that makes sense on its own and so could be a sentence in itself [e.g. The little girl shouted.]. A sentence always contains at least one main clause. It can contain more than one main clause if the clauses are linked with a co-ordinating conjunction [e.g. The little girl shouted <u>and</u> then she ran away.]. Lessons 21 and 22
- A **subordinate clause** is a less important clause that is added to a main clause, usually using a subordinating conjunction. It adds extra detail to the main clause [e.g. The little girl shouted <u>when she saw the wolf</u>.]. The subordinate clause 'when she saw the wolf' does not make sense without the main clause. Lesson 22

Comma

A **comma [,]** is a punctuation mark used to separate different parts of a sentence, for example:

- to separate the items in a list [e.g. She put the fresh eggs, a packet of cheese and some butter in the basket.]. Lesson 5
- to separate spoken words from non-spoken words in direct speech [e.g. "I'm hungry," he said.]. Lesson 16

Conjunction

A **conjunction** is a word that joins two words, phrases or clauses together. Conjunctions show how ideas link together [e.g. 'because' shows cause; 'when', 'while', and 'until' show time links; 'but' and 'although' show contrast]. Lessons 8, 9 and 10

There are two types of conjunction:

- **Co-ordinating conjunctions** [and, but, or] link together two words, phrases or clauses that are equally important [e.g. Bill <u>and</u> Diane were looking for a house <u>or</u> a flat. Bill preferred a house <u>but</u> Diane wanted a flat.]. Lesson 8
- **Subordinating conjunctions** [e.g. because; when; while] introduce a subordinate or less important clause [e.g. Bill preferred to live in a house <u>because</u> he wanted a garden.]. Lessons 8 and 22

Direct speech

Direct speech is when we record what someone says using the speaker's original words. Lessons 15 and 16

- **Inverted commas**, sometimes called **speech marks**, are used to mark the beginning and end of the spoken words [e.g. "My name is Jack."].
- Direct speech is often followed by a reporting clause [unspoken words that say who is speaking].
- A comma is placed within the inverted commas at the end of the spoken words [e.g. "My name is Jack," said the boy.]. Lessons 15 and 16
- If the spoken words are a question or an exclamation, then a question mark or exclamation mark is used instead of the comma [e.g. "What is your name?" asked the boy.]. Lesson 16

Heading and sub-heading
A **heading** is used to show the subject of the text that follows it [e.g. Staying healthy]. **Sub-headings** are used to show what each section or paragraph is about [e.g. Exercise; Diet]. Headings and sub-headings are used to organise ideas in writing. Lesson 23

Noun
Nouns are words that name things, people and places [e.g. car; park; man; day]. These are examples of **common nouns**.
- **Proper nouns** are the names of specific people, places and things [e.g. Joe Henson; Banbury Park; February]. Proper nouns start with a capital letter. Lesson 1
- A **noun phrase** is a group of words built around a noun. An expanded noun phrase might include a determiner, adjective[s], nouns and/or prepositional phrases [e.g. the fast police car with flashing lights]. Lesson 3
- A **compound noun** is a noun made up of two root words joined together [e.g. footpath; playground; skateboard.] Lesson 19
- An **abstract noun** is a noun that does not describe a person, place or thing but rather names an idea, quality, or state [e.g. bravery; willingness]. These words are often formed by adding suffixes such as –ness to adjectives. Lesson 19
- A **collective noun** refers to a whole group of things [e.g. a class of children]. Grammar 4

Paragraph
A **paragraph** is a group of sentences that go together because they have one main idea or theme. Paragraphs are used to organise ideas in writing. Lessons 23 and 24

Phrase
A **phrase** is a group of words that are connected together. Lesson 21
- A **noun phrase** is a group of words built around a noun. An expanded noun phrase might include a determiner, adjective[s], nouns and/or prepositional phrases [e.g. the fast police car with flashing lights]. Lesson 3
- A **prepositional phrase** is a group of words starting with a preposition [e.g. in the morning; under the bridge]. Lessons 13 and 14

Prefix
A **prefix** is a group of letters added to the start of an existing word to make another word. Adding a prefix changes the meaning of the original word. Some prefixes create negative meanings [e.g. undone; disagree]. Other prefixes have specific meanings [e.g. replay – 're–' means 'again'; submarine – 'sub–' means 'under']. Lesson 20

Preposition

A **preposition** is a word that shows how one thing relates to another in terms of place [e.g. <u>in</u> the bin; <u>behind</u> the tree; <u>from</u> the window], time [e.g. <u>before</u> dinner; <u>during</u> dinner; <u>after</u> dinner] or cause [e.g. <u>due to</u> the weather]. Lessons 13 and 14

A preposition is always followed by a noun, pronoun or noun phrase and this creates a **prepositional phrase** [e.g. before breakfast; before him; before the storm]. Lessons 13 and 14

Some words, including 'before', can act as prepositions or conjunctions. They are prepositions if they are followed by a noun, pronoun or noun phrase. They are conjunctions if followed by a clause.

Pronoun

A **pronoun** is a word that stands in place of a noun, proper noun or noun phrase. Lesson 28
- **Personal pronouns** are the most commonly used pronouns [e.g. I/me; he/him; they/them]. They help to avoid repetition. Lesson 28
- **Possessive pronouns** are used to show possession [e.g. This pencil is <u>mine</u>. That painting is <u>hers</u>.]. Grammar 4

Overuse of pronouns can lead to confusion about who or what the pronoun refers to. Grammar 4

Sentence

A **sentence** is a group of words put together to say something that makes sense. A sentence starts with a capital letter and ends with a full stop [.], question mark [?] or exclamation mark [!]. A sentence may consist of one clause or more than one clause. Sentences can be made longer by adding words, phrases and clauses that give more detail. Lessons 1 and 21

There are different forms of sentence with different functions and different grammatical patterns. Lesson 2
- **Statements** give information. They usually start with a subject followed by a verb [e.g. Joe ran away.].
- **Questions** ask for information and need a response. They can be formed using a question word [e.g. <u>What</u> is the weather like today?], a subject–verb reversal [e.g. <u>Is it</u> cold today?] or a question tag [e.g. It is cold today, <u>isn't it</u>?]. Questions always end with a question mark.
- **Commands** direct someone to do something. The main clause starts with a verb [e.g. Listen to me.].
- **Exclamations** express strong emotions and always end with an exclamation mark. A strict definition of an exclamation refers to sentences starting with 'What' or 'How' [e.g. What a surprise! How amazing!]. However, **interjections** are also exclamatory [e.g. Oh dear!]. Exclamation marks are sometimes added to other sentences to make exclamatory statements [e.g. It was great!] or exclamatory commands [e.g. Stop right there!]. However, this does not change the form of the sentence.

Sentence punctuation

Sentence punctuation refers to the use of capital letters and full stops to show the boundaries between sentences. It is an important part of punctuation as it helps to make the meaning of a text clear. Lesson 1
- A **question mark [?]** is used in place of a full stop if a sentence is a question. Lesson 2
- An **exclamation mark [!]** is used for exclamations or to show strong feeling. Lesson 2
- **Capital letters** are also used at the start of proper nouns and for the word 'I'. Lesson 1

Singular and plural

Many nouns have **singular** and **plural** forms. Singular means just one; plural means more than one. Many plurals are formed by adding –s or –es to the singular noun [e.g. cat<u>s</u>; dog<u>s</u>; fox<u>es</u>; lad<u>ies</u>]. However, some nouns have irregular plural forms [e.g. child – children; mouse – mice]. Some nouns are the same in the plural as they are in the singular [e.g. sheep; fish] and some nouns are always plural [e.g. scissors]. Non-countable nouns do not have a plural form [e.g. butter]. Lesson 30

Suffix

A **suffix** is a group of letters added to the end of an existing word to make another word. Suffixes often change words into different word classes [e.g. they are used to form adjectives – wonder<u>ful</u>, power<u>less</u>, fam<u>ous</u>; or to form nouns – kind<u>ness</u>, entertain<u>ment</u>]. Lesson 19

Verb

A **verb** is a 'doing' or 'being' word [e.g. He <u>ran</u>. He <u>is</u> sad.]. Verbs are important because they tell us about the actions in a sentence. They also show tense.
- **Tense (past and present)** Verbs usually have a tense. The tense tells us *when* the action happened – in the past or present. Many past-tense verbs are formed by adding –ed [e.g. waited; stopped; hurried]. Some verbs have irregular past-tense forms [e.g. see/saw; forget/forgot]. Lesson 17
- **Progressive forms** [also called continuous forms] can be used in the present and past tense to describe events that are, or were, in progress for some time. They use the –ing form of the verb with the helper [or auxiliary] verb 'am/are/is' in the present tense or 'was/were' in the past tense [e.g. He <u>is</u> singing. She <u>was</u> walk<u>ing</u>.]. Lesson 17
- **Perfect forms** are used to show time and cause relationships. The **present perfect form** of a verb is used to refer to events that began in the past but are still ongoing or still have consequences now [e.g. The tent has started to leak.]. It is formed using the helper [or auxiliary] verb 'has/have'. Lesson 18

Vowel and consonant

Vowels and **consonants** are the separate sounds that make up spoken words. In writing, these sounds are represented by letters or groups of letters. Lesson 4

Most of the letters in the alphabet represent consonant sounds. These are b c d f g h j k l m n p q r s t v w x y and z. Some vowel sounds are represented by the vowel letters a e i o and u. Other vowel sounds are represented by more than one letter [e.g. <u>ea</u>gle; <u>ar</u>m].

Word class

Every word belongs to a **word class**. The word class shows how the word is used. The main word classes are noun, verb, adjective, adverb, pronoun, conjunction, preposition and determiner. Lesson 27

- **Homonyms** are words that sound the same and are spelt the same but have different meanings. This means they can belong in different word classes. The context in which a word is used in a particular sentence determines its meaning and which word class it belongs to [e.g. He did <u>well</u>. He fetched water from the <u>well</u>.]. Lesson 27

Word family

Words in the same **word family** are related by meaning and how they are formed. They share the same root word [e.g. family, familiar] or a common root [e.g. horror, horrible]. Lessons 25 and 26

- A **root word** is a stand-alone word without any prefixes or suffixes added to it [e.g. 'build' is the root word of builder, rebuild, building.]. Lesson 25

KS2 English

Targeted Answer Book

Year 5

Grammar • Punctuation • Spelling

Contents

Grammar

Punctuation

Spelling

Published by CGP

ISBN: 978 1 78294 152 1
www.cgpbooks.co.uk
Clipart from Corel®
Printed by Elanders Ltd, Newcastle upon Tyne.
Based on the classic CGP style created by Richard Parsons.